Playing the Game

Playing
the
Game

liz ellis

A guide to playing netball

HarperSports
An imprint of HarperCollins*Publishers*

Harper*Sports*
An imprint of HarperCollins*Publishers*, Australia

First published in Australia in 2001
by HarperCollins*Publishers* Pty Ltd
ABN 36 009 913 517
A member of the HarperCollins*Publishers* (Australia) Pty Limited Group
http://www.harpercollins.com.au

HarperCollins*Publishers*
25 Ryde Road, Pymble, Sydney NSW 2073, Australia
31 View Road, Glenfield, Auckland 10, New Zealand
77–85 Fulham Palace Road, London W6 8JB, United Kingdom
Hazelton Lanes, 55 Avenue Road, Suite 2900, Toronto, Ontario M5R 3L2
and 1995 Markham Road, Scarborough, Ontario M1B 5M8, Canada
10 East 53rd Street, New York NY 10022, USA

National Library of Australia Cataloguing-in-Publication data:

Ellis, Liz.
Playing the game: a guide to playing netball.
ISBN 0 7322 6863 X.
1. Netball. I. Title.
796.324

Front cover picture: Newspix
Back cover pictures: John Sherwell/Netball Australia
Cover and internal design by Melanie Calabretta, HarperCollins Design Studio
Typeset by HarperCollins in 11/16 Ocean Sans Light
Printed and bound in Australia by Griffin Press on 79gsm Bulky Paperback White

7 6 5 4 3 2 1
04 03 02 01

Acknowledgements

When Alison Urquhart from HarperCollins approached me to write a book about how to play netball, I was flattered. But when I sat down at the computer, I got scared at the prospect of having to put everything I knew about netball into words. I also realised how much I didn't know about our great sport. So, I would like to thank those players who came to the rescue with information. Jenny Borlase, Vicki Wilson, Megan Anderson, Eloise Southby and Sharelle McMahon were all generous with their time. I'd like to give particular thanks to Cath Cox, Nerida Stuart and Karen Miller who all helped to write the shooting and centre-court chapters.

Thanks to Jill McIntosh for answering my many questions about scores, margins and the spelling of players' names. The Australian Netball Team support staff have also been of great assistance, with Kerry Leech, Paul Smith and Lindsay Ellis all willing to help me in the areas of nutrition, strength and conditioning training, and fitness testing respectively.

Alison and her team at HarperCollins have been fantastic. Their hard work and enthusiasm has seen this book grow from an idea, to pages of words, to the finished product without a hitch.

To my own support team a big thank you as well. To my agent Robert McMurtrie for his input into this book, the Liz Ellis Coaching Clinics and my career. To my family — Mum, Dad and my sister Kath — who have offered me so much encouragement, support and love without once putting pressure on me to succeed. And to my wonderful husband Matthew, who is my best friend and, when I am not playing netball, keeps my feet firmly on the ground.

I would also like to express my sincere gratitude to all of my netball coaches. I have been fortunate to have had some wonderful people guide my career. In particular, the late Sheila Eather, her daughter Raelene Kutzer, and Helen Lane in my junior days at Hawkesbury Netball Association, instilled in me a passion for netball and a desire to be the best player that I can be. Hopefully, the enthusiasm they had for the sport, which rubbed off on me, shows through in this book.

Contents

Chapter 1

That Game

'NO! The penalty goes against Ellis. Twenty seconds on the clock and Ellis is stood out of play. New Zealand shoot for the match. NO — it's a miss! Ellis, Ellis, Ellis hauls in the rebound. Australia run it down court — they need to score. Forty-one [goals] apiece. There is a turnover. No, Tombs gets it. The timekeeper is up. Forty-one apiece. Australia with a late charge. McMahon, McMahon shoots, she's got it, she's got it! Sharelle McMahon has won the match for Australia. Unbelievable scenes here in Christchurch. This is one of the greatest sporting performances by any team on this planet!'

Whether Mark Aiston's commentary with Anne Sargeant of the 1999 World Netball Championship final is entirely accurate or not is a matter of debate amongst sports fans. At the very least, Aiston's final comment can be attributed to his being caught up in the emotion of the moment. At most, it can be described as an honest assessment of a game that brought tears to the eyes of the spectators — even those who had never watched a netball game before. The last twenty seconds of commentary from Aiston and Sargeant capture the essence of that final. The championship belonged to the team who could pot the winning goal in the dying seconds of the match. Both teams had their opportunities, but only one team had Sharelle McMahon. Thankfully, she was playing for Australia.

Without a doubt, that game was the greatest moment in my sporting career. There is nothing quite like the thrill of pitting your skills against one of the best netball teams in the world and winning. Let alone winning the final of the World Netball Championships in such a dramatic fashion. Even now, I get goosebumps whenever any footage of that match is played, and I get tears in my eyes when I watch the last twenty seconds of the game, listen to the commentary and see the absolute joy on our faces when we realised what we had done.

I have not tired of talking about 'that match' to anyone who wants to listen, and, in my sillier moments, I am even happy to give a re-enactment of the way my team-mates and I celebrated by rolling on the ground after the final whistle was blown. The thing that made that particular victory so special for us was the manner in which the match was won.

I was a part of the Australian team that competed in the 1995 World Netball Championships. That year, we successfully defended Australia's World Championship title with a twenty-goal victory over South Africa in the final. (In 1991, the Australian team had won with a one-goal thriller against New Zealand.) The 1995 World Championship was my first, which made the win a special one for me, but I knew from looking at the faces of my team-mates that the 1995 final did not elicit the same feelings as the emotion-charged victory four years ago. Sure, we had overcome a determined New Zealand side by a single goal (once again) in a round match, and that was a great game. But it wasn't the final. While the members of the South African team, who were fresh onto the international competition scene following the lifting of the sporting ban on their country, fought valiantly until the final whistle, it was still a twenty-goal victory. What the result would be at the end of the 1995 final was evident by the start of the last quarter — Australia would be the 1995 World Netball Champions.

Don't get me wrong — I was still excited, as were our legions of fans back home, who kicked and screamed until the NSW Government granted us a ticker-tape parade through the streets of Sydney when we returned. For me, that was a particularly proud moment, as we were (and still are) the only female sporting team to be granted this honour in Sydney. In 1999, when we returned successful from the World Championships, we were honoured in this way again.

Which brings me back to the 1999 final and the way we won it. In a nutshell, the victory was so special because we weren't supposed to win it. From the moment the Australian team arrived in New Zealand we were bombarded with reports of how good the Silver Ferns were. According to the press, they had the right blend of youth, experience and skill to take the title from Australia, whereas we were a team past our prime (our average age was twenty-eight). On the day we arrived in New Zealand, the headline in the *Sunday Star Times* was 'Jill's Geriatrics'. 'Jill' referred to our coach, Jill McIntosh, and the reference to 'Geriatrics' — well, go figure! We felt that as reigning Commonwealth Games and World Champions, we deserved a little more respect.

Sure, New Zealand were good — we saw that for ourselves when we watched their earlier round matches. They were an extremely well-drilled team. From the start of their warm-up through to the final whistle, they looked like they knew where they were going to pass the ball before they had even caught it. This, combined with a formidable back line led by Bernice Mene, made the Silver Ferns a very impressive unit. Add to this the fact that they had handed us a twelve-goal defeat at the start of the year in the Fisher & Paykel Plate, and we knew the Silver Ferns deserved to start the 1999 final as favourites. But all of these factors did not make them unbeatable. There is no such thing as an unbeatable side.

The Silver Ferns were the more impressive team in the lead-up games. They had posted some big scores in their round matches against high-calibre teams such as South Africa and Trinidad and Tobago. The Silver Ferns had also survived the semi-final the night before against Jamaica, where in a physically gruelling match, the Silver Ferns had triumphed by just two points.

On the other hand, Australia did not come through our round matches as impressively as New Zealand. We had good wins against Jamaica and England, two of the top four teams in the competition, but we failed to post really big wins against some of the lesser-ranked teams. For some reason, prior to the final, our game hadn't come together as well as we had hoped. Our team had a bad habit of playing blistering netball in some quarters, and then looking like we had never played with each other in other quarters. This was through no lack of trying, but sometimes things don't gel when you want them to. Personally, I went into the final feeling that I had not played my best netball during the tournament.

To an impartial spectator, all these factors may have led to the conclusion that Australia would not pose a serious threat to New Zealand's planned domination of the 1999 World Netball Championships. To have reached such a conclusion, however, would not have taken into account the passion we feel when we represent Australia, and the pride we feel when we run onto the court wearing green and gold. These emotions are things that cannot be measured by experts — or underestimated by our opposition. They come from within each player and join the team together with a common and unique bond. The pride I feel when I am granted the rare privilege of representing my country cannot be adequately described — nor can the phenomenon that makes Australian players taller, faster and stronger when it counts.

On the day of the final, I promised myself that I would not walk off that court until I had run, jumped, passed and thrown myself into physical and mental exhaustion. I promised myself that I would do whatever it took to play my part in winning the final.

When I was a hopeful twenty year old trying to break into the Australian team, I had a conversation with Jenny Borlase after the 1991 World Championships. Jenny had been a member of the 1991 team and I was firing questions at her about their preparation for the match. When I asked her whether the team had any idea that the 1991 final would be the thriller it was, Jen replied that on the morning of that game, their coach, Joyce Brown, out of the blue said, 'Tonight is going to be a very special night.' As is Joyce's habit, she was right. When I recalled that conversation, I sincerely hoped that the 1999 final would turn out to be a game that would be held up there with the 1991 final — a game I had watched as part of the capacity crowd at the Sydney Entertainment Centre and which inspired me to want to play for Australia one day.

The 1999 final was the most intense game of netball I have ever played. Right from the very first whistle, bodies hit the ground more often than the ball hit the sweet spot of the goal ring. It was tough, it was physical, and it was a classic trans-Tasman battle. The first quarter was an even affair — both teams went into the break with thirteen goals apiece after the lead changed hands several times throughout the quarter. The second quarter was much the same as the first, although New Zealand had managed to sneak a two-goal lead by the half-time break. What I remember most about the first half of that game is that none of the goalers on the court could find their range. Vicki Wilson, our captain and the undisputed queen of the goal circle until this match, was missing goals she would normally shoot with her eyes shut. I should know, she had landed enough goals against me when I played opposite her in the Commonwealth Bank Trophy. At the other end of the court, Silver Fern Donna Loffhagen had also been uncharacteristically inaccurate with her shooting.

At half time it occurred to me that the winning team would most likely be the one that could get its goalers to fire first. I wanted to tell Vicki and her partner in the goal circle, Jacqui Delaney, that our fate rested in their hands — as if they didn't know that already! Fortunately, there were enough people who actually knew what they were talking about who were giving Vicki and Jacqui advice, so I kept my mouth shut and instead willed them to find their range. As a humble defender, the only thing I could have said was 'Get your goals in', and that's probably not the best thing to say to a goal shooter during the half-time break of a World Netball Championships final!

The third quarter was an absolute nightmare for us. To my horror, it was the Kiwi goalers who found their range first, with my opponent Donna Loffhagen going from a 69 per cent conversion rate to an amazing — and for me, heartbreaking — 90 per cent. As a result, we started the final quarter of the game with a six-goal deficit. It was an almost insurmountable margin. All I knew was that we had to do our best.

In hindsight, it seems fitting that 'Whatever it Takes' was our motto for the 1999 season. Certainly, Jill McIntosh reinforced that motto during the final break. She told us that we were to go out there and do whatever it took to win that final. We also had new personnel in our shooting line-up — Sharelle McMahon and Jenny Borlase replaced Vicki Wilson and Jacqui Delaney respectively. It must have been an incredibly hard decision for Jill to replace our captain in Vicki's final match for Australia. Unfortunately for Vicki, she played, in her own words, 'a dog of a game'. I would not have been so harsh — she had certainly shown flashes of the form that had made her one of the most respected goalers in the world. Nevertheless, Vicki's third-quarter shooting statistics necessitated the change of line-up. It wasn't a fairytale end to her magnificent career, but I have no doubt that it won't be her shooting statistics in the 1999 final that Vicki will be remembered for, but rather the amazing netball she produced while playing for Australia and Queensland during her top-level career, which spanned some seventeen years.

While it was a blow to the team to lose our captain for the final quarter, Jill was right to rejig the line-up, and we had every confidence in the new shooting partnership of Jenny and Sharelle. Jenny Borlase had been playing for Australia for almost a decade and Sharelle had the experience of the 1998 Commonwealth Games final under her belt, where we had come back from a four-goal deficit in the dying minutes of the game to snatch the gold medal from New Zealand.

Could we repeat our Commonwealth Games performance? That was the question only we could answer. Since the World Championship final, I have spoken to many people who had written us off at the start of the last quarter. Even those hardy souls with green and gold face paint who had ventured into the arena filled with 8000 screaming New Zealanders must have had their doubts. We had not won a single quarter in the match — so what chance did we have of winning the last one by seven goals?

Out of all the people sitting in the stadium that night, and those around the world who were watching the final on television or listening on the radio, it is possible that there were only eighteen who believed that we could do it — the Australian team and our support staff. While in our huddle at three-quarter time, Jill reminded us of all of the hard work we had done to get to this point, and that if we let the game go now, it would be an absolute waste of our hard work and collective talent. She put it in simple terms — we only needed three turnovers to even the score. She reminded us to concentrate on doing the simple things well — to focus on the process of the game rather than its outcome.

The final quarter was dominated by physical clashes and desperate defence from both teams. The last three minutes were mind blowing. I kept reminding myself to stay calm and to do the little things well. However, it was very difficult to remain calm when I gave away a penalty under the post with twenty seconds on the clock. The scores were even and if Donna Loffhagen had sunk that shot, it would have been all over — there would not have been enough time left for us to take our centre pass and score.

As Donna took the shot, I kept in mind that she had missed two similar shots during the previous few minutes. I promised myself that if that ball bounced off the ring, no one but me was going to get it in her hands. When that shot did bounce and I got it, I had the immediate problem of what to do with it. I am not known for my ball-handling abilities, so I was glad to get rid of it — and even gladder to see Carissa Tombs and Kath Harby take the ball down the court.

My whole world nearly fell apart when Shelley O'Donnell slipped and lost possession of the ball, but it was saved by Carissa Tombs who, looking like she had all the time in the world, ambled over and picked up the ball and passed it on to Sharelle McMahon. Sharelle decided that five seconds left on the clock was far too much time to have spare, and she passed the ball out to Shelley and found a better position in the circle to shoot from. Down at the other end of the court, I decided I might cause her grievous bodily harm if she didn't take a shot in the next few seconds. I also remember thinking that I didn't have it in me to play extra time, so when Sharelle turned, took aim, and shot that last goal oh-so-sweetly, I was happy just to roll around on the floor in delirium.

Looking back at that game, it's clear that Sharelle had no idea of what she had just done. In her mind, she had shot just another goal and started to run back to the line — while picking her undies out of her bum — to get ready for the next centre pass. It was this action of Sharelle's that sums up those last few moments of the 1999 World Netball Championships final. We focused on the simple things. While I haven't spoken to Donna Loffhagen about that last shot she took and missed, and so could not presume to know what her thoughts were, it seemed to me that she was shooting to win the World Championships, whereas Sharelle was shooting just another goal. And there lies the key to our success — we were process, rather than outcome, driven. I think the Silver Ferns went on to the court in the final quarter seeking to win the World Championships. We went on aiming to win fifteen minutes of netball by seven goals. In my mind, our goal was much easier to achieve.

This, however, may be an overly academic assessment of the win — there may have been another factor to that final. My extended family had gathered in Sydney to watch the game. By three-quarter time they had tried everything to get us going. They had yelled, screamed and sworn at the television. They had jumped up and down and pulled their hair out. Yet there we were, six goals down. During the commercial break between the third and fourth quarters there were glum faces all around as my family sat in a Sydney lounge room, feeling pretty helpless as they watched us slip further and further behind. There was nothing they could do — was there? Suddenly, one of my cousins had a brain wave. The only thing they hadn't done was pray — so why not give it a go? But what to say in a prayer for the Australian Netball Team? Everyone turned to look at the one person who could help them. Sister Anne was an old family friend who had been invited along to watch the telecast of the final. Surely, a nun would know what to say. Sister Anne didn't miss a beat. She made the sign of the cross, clasped her hands together in prayer and said, 'Hail Mary, full of Grace, please put the ball in the right place.' Fifteen minutes later, we were the netball champions of the world.

Whether our win was due to divine intervention or to our ability to remain focused on the process rather than the outcome is a matter for conjecture. After the final whistle, all I cared about was that we had won. I remember looking into Kath Harby's eyes and both of us screaming. Total disbelief, total relief, total excitement, tears, hugging, more screaming, more tears. In our delirious celebrations, the Australian Netball Team — made up of women who were bank officers, school teachers, engineers, mothers, dental therapists, sponsorship managers and lawyers — lost all sense of decorum and we rolled around together on the floor. It was an unbelievable feeling.

Recently, I had a conversation with Sharelle McMahon about those moments after we won. We agreed that we would have loved to have been able to bottle that feeling of jubilation so that we could pull it out occasionally, just to savour the moment. Of course, we couldn't do that, so we will be forced to spend the remainder of our netball careers trying to re-create that moment. So if you see me running around the netball court when I am eighty years old, don't laugh — I am still chasing that feeling!

Chapter 2

In the Beginning

My initial forays into netball were not as glorious as the 1999 World Netball Championships final!

By the age of eight, I hadn't shown much interest in sport. My interests centred around reading voraciously and teasing my little sister Kath (both of which are still favourite pastimes of mine). I was not an overly coordinated child, and this, combined with my bookworm habits and preference for spending time in my own little dreamworld, did not suggest to my parents that I might like to take up any sport — let alone a team sport!

So there I was, happily reading and dreaming and teasing Kath, when one of Mum's friends called her and mentioned that they needed a few more girls to make up an under-nine team and asked her if I would like to start playing netball. Mum, in her infinite wisdom, politely declined the invitation on the basis that she didn't think I would like netball. Fortunately, my mother's friend was not put off by Mum's feeble protests, and she called back the next day and informed Mum that she had read in the newspaper about a study that found that a high percentage of 'juvenile delinquents' had never played team sports, and that Mum was risking my future by not giving me the chance to play netball.

I have absolutely no idea why Mum thought I was in danger of becoming a juvenile delinquent, but quicker than you can say 'goal keeper', I was registered in the Green Hills Netball Club under-nine team. In no time at all, I was spending an inordinate amount of time on my bum and knees every Saturday morning as I struggled to come to terms with limbs that were longer than I realised — and which seemed to have a mind of their own.

Despite my initial affinity with the asphalt surface of the court, I loved netball from the moment I threw my first chest pass. Initially, I was put into centre because I was the biggest and bossiest and I liked to hog the ball. I moved from there to goal attack when I realised that there was more glory in shooting goals than delivering the ball to the goalers. This was a pretty good position — until I came to the unhappy realisation that I couldn't shoot when someone was defending me. So I packed my bag and headed for the defence line.

When I was first told to play goal keeper, I cried. I thought that it was the most useless position to play. Little did I realise that goal keeper is one of the most demanding and thankless positions on the court, but enormously satisfying when things are going my way. (Which is not as often as I would like!)

Even now, goal keeper is a much-maligned position. Whenever I run coaching clinics, very few girls want to own up to playing goal keeper, until I say that only the smart, pretty and nice girls can play this position. After that, the number of hands in the air asking for the goal keeper bib usually quadruples!

Possibly the only drawback I encountered during my early years of playing netball was the recurrent asthma attacks I suffered on cold Saturday mornings. After being diagnosed as a severe asthmatic as an infant, my parents duly gave me all of the required medications but told me that I was only a mild asthmatic and that I shouldn't let it bother me too much. It wasn't until I was selected to play in the Australian Netball Team some fifteen years later that, following a routine medical, our doctor informed me that based upon my medical history and what she had observed of me, I was in fact a severe asthmatic. My parents later confirmed this. Mum and Dad explained that at the suggestion of our family doctor, they had not made a big deal out of my condition. This was to ensure that I would never feel that I had a disability of any sort and to allow me to live my life without thinking that being an asthmatic would hold me back. As it turns out, it was a stroke of genius, and as a result, I have never felt hampered by my asthma. Sure, it bothers me sometimes, but I have never felt that being an asthmatic has stopped me from pursuing my sport.

So how does a tall, gawky, asthmatic bookworm playing for Green Hills in the under-nines competition at Windsor get to play for Australia at the World Netball Championships? That is the question I am most frequently asked. It is also the hardest question to answer simply. Essentially, it is a matter of setting yourself goals and then doing the work to reach them — although that is not what I was doing as a nine-year-old kid with scabby knees!

The best way to describe my path from Green Hills under-nines to the Australian Netball Team is that it was like a long staircase. If I had stood at the bottom and focused only on the top, it would have seemed like an awfully long way to climb. However, I focused on climbing each little step one at a time, and I found myself getting closer and closer to my ultimate goal. For me, the first few steps were climbed when I was selected to play in the Hawkesbury under-age teams. Although initially, it was a case of two steps forward and one step back, these teams were vital to my development as a netball player.

The first time I realised that I might be a reasonable netball player was when I was selected to play in the Hawkesbury under-eleven representative team for the State Championships. It was so exciting — not because I was selected to play representative netball for the first time, but because it meant that I got to play netball for three whole days in a row!

I thought that playing representative netball was great fun, and I couldn't wait until the following year when I could do it all again. Unfortunately, I was to learn that you can never take selection into any representative team for granted. My first major netball disappointment came at the ripe old age of eleven when I missed out on selection in the Hawkesbury under-twelve team. I cried myself to sleep that night and vowed that I would make the team the following year. Much to the relief of my family, who had to put up with me being miserable for weeks afterwards, I was called into the team at late notice when one of the other players withdrew due to injury. I made sure that I trained harder than the other girls to ensure I never missed selection again. It paid off and I was selected the following year and in each of my junior years after that.

The next few steps were selection into the New South Wales under-sixteen and open Catholic Schoolgirls teams between 1987 and 1990. While being selected into schoolgirls teams is not absolutely essential to progress up the netball staircase, it certainly gave me valuable experience playing representative netball and it exposed me to high-calibre coaches such as Maria Lynch, who was my coach when I was in the NSW under-seventeen team.

Another of my coaches when I played Catholic Schoolgirls was Kerry Lambley. Kerry was a tough taskmaster who believed that at the under-sixteen National Catholic Schoolgirls Championships, we were taking too long to get into games. To combat this problem, she took the dramatic step of waking us up at 5.00 am on the morning of our final to run a few laps around the oval in our pyjamas and to do half an hour of ball work. Afterwards, still bewildered, we stumbled back to bed. We woke up a couple of hours later wondering if it had all been a dream. Fortunately, it hadn't and we won the final that afternoon after setting up the win with a blistering first quarter!

In 1989, I took a few more steps up the staircase when I was selected to be a member of the NSW under-seventeen team. Our coach, Maria Lynch, like Kerry Lambley, commanded our respect as a hard taskmaster. We were an incredibly well-drilled team, and under Maria's tutelage, we were ready to take on the best sixteen year olds the rest of Australia could throw at us! The first game I played for the NSW under-seventeens was memorable for me not because we won or because I played well, but because every time I got an intercept or took a throw-in, I managed to throw the ball to one of the opposition. Maria decided that the only way to deal with my problem was with the brutal truth and at quarter time, in front of the rest of the team, she reminded me that I was playing in the team that had the blue uniform on, and asked if I wouldn't mind throwing the ball to one of those players. I was terribly embarrassed but it worked. While I am not the best in the business when it comes to ball disposal, I haven't had such a horrible start to a game since — although my first game for Australia came close. That game was against Wales, and my first four intercepts found their way straight back into the opposition's hands. Needless to say, my coach at the time, Joyce Brown, gave me a similar message to the one Maria had given me all those years ago — only Joyce was less polite!

In 1990, I was selected as part of the NSW under-nineteen team. This step was significant because the team was coached by Julie Fitzgerald, whose Ku-ring-gai team I decided to join following my return from the Australian Institute of Sport (AIS) at the end of 1992. Julie is still my coach at the Swifts. Her strength as a coach is unusual in that she believes that we need to have other things in our lives apart from netball in order to play well. She cares about our lives first and our netball second. This is a refreshing approach to coaching, and it is nice to know that there is a degree of flexibility in training so that the netball season is a positive outlet, rather than a weight around our necks. If, for example, we are super-tired or stressed or have a lot on our plates at work, then it is no drama for us to skip training. This, of course, is with the understanding that we work doubly hard at the next session. Nobody abuses this system, as we know that non-attendance at training is detrimental not only to our personal performances, but also to that of the team. It does help to know, though, that our coach is just as interested in our mental well-being as our physical.

My time at the AIS from 1991 to 1992 was responsible for my biggest steps up the representative staircase. Under the expert supervision of Head Coach and former Australian representative Gaye Teede, I embarked on an enormous learning curve. It wasn't long before I realised that I had an awful lot of work to do to be even considered for the Australian Netball Team. When I turned up on the doorstep of the AIS in 1991, I was there largely because of my natural ability and the skills I had learnt from my various coaches. Up until this point, I had never embarked on a weights program, never cared about what I ate, and I couldn't have run out of sight on a dark night. As for sprints — they were what you did to beat your sister to the front seat of the car, weren't they?

During my first week at the AIS, we were subjected to a battery of fitness tests. You name it, it was measured — height, weight, percentage body fat (taken as a measurement of skinfolds over several sites around the body), speed, vertical jump, agility and endurance. About the only test I got a reasonable result in was height!

Even though I was quite lean, I didn't have much muscle. That would change. I learnt that I had to eat foods high in carbohydrates and protein, which helped me to build up some muscle bulk and provided much-needed energy. If I had remained as I was, I would have been pushed around in elite competition. As for my speed, agility and endurance — they needed a lot of work.

Speed and agility were addressed by a program designed specifically for netball players, which the whole squad followed. Our weights sessions were carried out under the watchful eyes of the AIS strength and conditioning coaches, and our endurance sessions usually took place at 6.30 am on cold Canberra mornings. I am not a naturally fit person, nor am I a great runner. Combine these things with my tendency to wheeze when the temperature drops, and it's no surprise that I learnt to dread fitness sessions! Despite my dread, I knew that there could be no chickening out. If I wanted to make the Australian Netball Team one day, I had to do what they did. I was determined to get fitter, stronger and faster.

Gradually, I managed to improve all these areas of my fitness. I even began to like fitness sessions, and I almost looked forward to the testing so I could see whether I had improved.

For two years, my life revolved around morning fitness sessions, daytime weights sessions and afternoon netball training. I also managed to embark on a combined degree in Arts and Law at the Australian National University, which I later completed at Macquarie University in Sydney. The AIS wasn't all hard work, and I did manage to have some time to hone my social skills. I made some wonderful friends while I was there, and although many of the girls in the 1991 and 1992 AIS netball squads are my opponents on-court, we are all mates off-court.

At the end of my first year at the AIS, I was named as one of the Australian Open Netball Squad. This was a squad of twenty players from which the 1992

Australian Netball Team would be chosen. I was pretty nervous when I went to my first training camp, because I would be expected to keep pace with players who were netball goddesses in my eyes. Women like Keeley Devery, Vicki Wilson, Michelle Den Dekker (then Fielke) and Catriona Wagg would soon be passing the ball to me — little Lizzy Ellis from Windsor, the nine year old with the scabby knees (that's how I felt at least) — and, heaven forbid, I would have to catch it!

I was petrified, but I was also absolutely determined to impress my heroes. In our first session of match play, I was playing against Jenny Borlase, goal shooter extraordinaire. As the ball came towards us I started to move my feet, hoping against all hope to get an intercept — or at least a tip — and show everyone that I was worthy of being there. The result? I fell over, the ball whistled by and Jenny shot a routine goal. I had managed to impress the other squad members, but not in the way I had hoped. Instead of admiring my skills, everyone was impressed with the novel way the new girl had found of falling over her own feet and landing flat on her face.

Fortunately for my rather battered ego, the only way to go from my inauspicious beginning was up, and within two years I had won selection into the Australian Open Team to contest the World Games in The Hague. I received limited court time on that particular tour — I played only one game in the six-match tournament — but I benefited greatly from touring with some of the best netballers in the world. The fact that I didn't get much court time didn't really bother me. Even though I would have loved to have played more games, it was such a thrill to be part of the Australian Netball Team that I was content to use my first tour to learn as much as I could both from the players and from coach Joyce Brown. I tried to sit on the bench so that I was within earshot of Joyce, and I was always on the lookout for some titbit of information that I could file away. As a result, I came back from that tour a more knowledgeable player. I also came back with a determination to work harder than ever before and to force my way into the starting line, which I did the following year.

This chapter is not an exhaustive list of all of the steps I took during my long climb to the Australian Netball Team. On the contrary, these are just some of the bigger ones. I took smaller steps on a monthly, weekly and even a daily basis. Mastering a new skill in training or adding another facet to my game (such as extra speed or an increased vertical jump) represents a small but important step. I still have goals that I want to achieve, such as winning the Commonwealth Bank Trophy and playing for Australia in a third World Netball Championship, and I hope to do these things by taking a few small steps at a time. The key to getting where you want to be is not to get disillusioned because you think that your ultimate goal is so far away. Simply set yourself little goals, and each time you achieve them, you are that extra step closer to your ultimate dream.

This method of achieving your goals is not something that is limited to netball. It can be applied across all fields of endeavour, whether it be school, university, work, or saving for a new bike! When I was younger, my dad used to say, 'If you look after the pennies, the pounds will look after themselves.' I think this is true when you are trying to achieve anything worthwhile. If you take care of the small things, they will soon become part of something much bigger.

Chapter 3

Other Highlights

Between being selected for the Australian team for the first time in 1993 and winning the World Championships final in 1999, there have been many memorable moments in my career as an elite netball player.

Probably the biggest ongoing thrill I get is running out onto the court wearing the Australian uniform and singing the national anthem. If you watch the Australian team at a test match, you will see that I am not alone in this. We all know the words to the anthem and we are not afraid to sing them!

Coming in a close second to our World Championship win in 1999 was our performance at the Commonwealth Games in Kuala Lumpur in 1998. This game ranks as a highlight in my career, not only because it was another classic trans-Tasman thriller, but also because it was incredibly special to be part of something bigger than a netball tournament. We were part of a bigger team of athletes, all of us competing for our country. As netball is not an Olympic sport, the Commonwealth Games is our one opportunity to be part of a wider celebration of sport.

It was absolutely mind blowing to arrive in the athletes' village on a humid September day in 1998. There were athletes there from all around the globe, of all shapes, sizes and colours. The number of countries there was brought home to me at the opening ceremony, which was an amazing experience.

The brand new stadium, purpose built for the games, was packed full of cheering people. As the games were in Malaysia, the biggest roar was, of course, reserved for the home team. Nevertheless, the atmosphere was amazing as we walked onto the running track and did a full lap of the stadium. I felt as if we broke the world record for the four hundred metres — our lap seemed to pass so quickly. I was disappointed when we found ourselves in front of the athletes' seating area — I had so much more waving and smiling to do!

We made full use of our time at the Commonwealth Games. Our coach, Jill McIntosh, allowed us plenty of opportunity to take in the atmosphere and other sporting events. We even managed to wriggle our way into the swimming venue on the night the Australian swimmers won every event and finished it off by breaking the world record in the final event — the men's 4 x 100m freestyle relay.

As the final of the Commonwealth Games netball competition drew closer, we began to curtail our extra-curricular activities and started to focus on the task at hand. Having already had a good look at the wider sporting spectacle going on around us, we were able to put that distraction aside and focus on our goal — winning the Commonwealth Games gold medal for the first time that netball had been a Commonwealth Games sport.

We had a pretty good run through our pool — we overcame Malaysia, Barbados, Jamaica, England and Canada. The semi-final saw us playing against South Africa, the 1995 World Championships finalists, who we defeated as part of our march to the gold medal match. Our opponents in the final were our old enemy, New Zealand. We had beaten the Silver Ferns comfortably in a three-test series earlier in the year. In that series, the closest they got to us was eleven goals in the final match. Based upon these earlier results, it would have been easy to assume that we were virtually assured of a gold medal.

But in international competition, it is best not to assume anything and, instead, do some thorough research about your opposition. We watched some of the Silver Ferns' early games, and it didn't take long for us to come to the conclusion that they were a vastly improved team from the one we had beaten earlier in the year. They were moving the ball down the court with much more authority and confidence than we had seen in a long time, and it seemed to me that their defence end was gaining an enormous amount of possession for their front line to capitalise on.

We knew that to beat the Silver Ferns in the final, we would have to play a short, sharp game in attack in order to work our way through their defensive zone. This style of defence, which is characteristic of the New Zealand team, is aimed at combating the fast ball movement down the court which Australia does so well. Essentially, the players defend a particular 'space' rather than a player, which allows them to intercept any long, cross-court or floating passes.

In defence, we had to ensure that we didn't allow the Silver Ferns' attack line to settle into any sort of rhythm, and so our focus was on shutting down their space and putting plenty of pressure over the ball.

The night before our final also happened to be the second last night of the Commonwealth Games. As a result, we had a fairly restless night since many of the other athletes in the village were celebrating the end of their events. I recall laying in bed at about 4.00 am, after being woken by a party going on somewhere in the village and thinking that I wanted to win the gold medal so desperately that I didn't care if I had to do it with only a couple of hours of sleep behind me. So, rather than worrying about not being able to sleep, I lay there and visualised the team receiving our gold medals and singing the anthem. In my mind, I took intercepts and grabbed rebounds and helped Australia become the first ever Commonwealth Games gold medallists for netball.

I must have fallen asleep thinking these positive thoughts because the next thing I knew, it was 7.00 am and time to get out of bed and get ready. This was the least enjoyable part of the Commonwealth Games. Because the netball competition was part of a much larger event, our scheduled playing times were a little different to what we were used to. During our Commonwealth Bank Trophy season, games never start before 7.30 pm and even at World

Championships, where there are a lot of games to get through daily, we generally don't have to play before about 2.00 pm. At the Commonwealth Games, however, it was a totally different story. Our games were generally scheduled for the morning, and the grand final was no exception.

The match was down to begin at 11.30 am. We needed to arrive at the venue at about 10.00 am to give the goalers time to practise at the posts and allow the rest of us to carry out our pre-game routine, as well as having a good thirty minutes spare for us to warm up. As the netball venue was about forty-five minutes drive from the village, we had to leave at 8.30 am, to allow for travel time and possible traffic delays, which in turn necessitated an early rise in order to have breakfast, strap our ankles, pack our kit bags and get ready to leave. Needless to say, it wasn't the best preparation for someone who is not, by any stretch of the imagination, a morning person.

Nevertheless, we knew that if we were struggling with the early rise then our opponents would be as well. If we wanted the gold medal, we would have to overcome whatever challenges arose along the way.

Despite the early hour, both teams managed to produce netball that was worthy of the first Commonwealth Games netball final. We struggled to find our attacking rhythm early on, thanks to some superb defensive pressure from the Silver Ferns. Similarly, the New Zealand combination of Donna Loffhagen and Belinda Colling failed to find their marks early, and as a result, by the quarter-time break, both teams were level with twelve goals apiece.

We intensified our effort during the second quarter. Our defence was stronger and the attacking line started to find its range in the final few minutes. We had a five-goal lead by half time, with a score of 24–19. At this point, Jill McIntosh decided to remove Vicki Wilson from the game in order to inject something new into the front end. As she would do with so much aplomb a year later at the World Championships, Jenny Borlase was called upon to slot some goals for us.

This new combination didn't fire, and within seven minutes the Silver Ferns had reduced our half-time lead, and the game was level at twenty-eight-all. Fortunately for us, the Kiwis called time for an injury to Donna Loffhagen, which gave us a little bit of breathing space. Jill seized the opportunity to bring

Vicki Wilson back into the line and returned Jenny to the sideline. The break had certainly fired Vicki up, and although we did not rebuild our previous lead during this quarter, the rhythm of our game returned and by the end of the third quarter, we were even with the Silver Ferns at 31–31.

The three-quarter time break was memorable for the words from our veteran wing defence, Simone McKinnis. Simone had not yet made a public announcement about her future in netball, but the team knew that this final was to be her last ever game of netball. Simone had played for her country on sixty-six previous occasions, and she drew upon this experience to fire us up for the last fifteen minutes of the game. In just a few words, she recapped on the hard work we had done to get to this point, and she summed up with a reminder that we had not been through so much only to falter now. Simone's language was incredibly emotive, and she got the message through to us. She had drawn her line in the sand and she was going to drag us over it no matter what. I think Simone used every ounce of energy she had for those last fifteen minutes. In fact, I think she mortgaged some of her future energy and well-being as well. The next day, she could barely walk on legs that, twenty-four hours previously, had run, jumped and bounded their owner through a gruelling netball final.

Simone's words did the trick — albeit not immediately. Even though we had started to get our act together at the end of the third quarter, we did not begin the final quarter in the same fashion. With a couple of early turnovers, the Silver Ferns got away to a two-goal lead — a lead they managed to hold on to until the last seven minutes of the match. When we lost the ball off our centre pass — which, had they scored, would have given the Silver Ferns a three-goal lead with their centre to come — it seemed that our chance at Commonwealth Games glory was lost.

As the ball came down the court, I remember yelling 'NO'. I didn't aim my protest at anyone in particular, but it was a catalyst for some defensive action. Simone McKinnis, goal defence Kath Harby and I defended our hearts out and won the ball back. It was like a switch had been flicked, and in the final seven minutes we scored nine goals to New Zealand's four and took the match 42–39. It was an incredibly emotional moment. For all of us, it meant so much to be the first netball team to win a Commonwealth Games gold medal. It was a fitting end to Simone McKinnis's career, and, as we would later discover, to the international careers of Nicole Cusack and Sarah Sutter.

The Commonwealth Games final also marked the emergence of Sharelle McMahon as a new star of Australian netball. Sharelle, with only one year of Commonwealth Bank Trophy experience behind her, was catapulted into the senior ranks when she was selected for our tour of the Caribbean at the start of 1998. She underwent an incredibly successful baptism of fire when she was given her first taste of international netball when she was put on at half time in the third test match against Jamaica in Kingstown. We had lost the first test, and won the second comfortably, but we found ourselves two goals down at half time in the third — we were dangerously close to losing our first test series in almost a decade. Rather than wilt under the pressure of being thrown onto the court to play for Australia for the first time in front of a patriotic Jamaican crowd and against a physically tough team, Sharelle held her composure and helped lift Australia to a one-goal win to clinch the series. Sharelle had grown in confidence and ability with every outing that year, and she finished off with a great performance as part of our gold medal-winning team. In doing so, she forced one of Australia's stars onto the bench. Nicole Cusack had been one of Australia's best goal attacks during the nineties, and it must have been incredibly difficult for her to come to terms with finishing her career on the sidelines. What was so impressive about Nicole's off-court performance at the Commonwealth Games was the fact that she put the team's needs before her own. Nicole, Sharelle and I shared a room for the three weeks we were in Kuala Lumpur. It was a testament to both Nicole's and Sharelle's character that there was never any ill feeling between them over what was happening on the court. They both fought incredibly hard to stake their claim as goal attack, but this rivalry never affected their ability to get along with each other. As their roomy, I was grateful for that (even if I didn't like their taste in music!).

The Australian team celebrated that gold medal win well into the night. However, our revelries were limited to the athletes' village, as we were advised to steer well clear of the city due to some civil unrest. Little did we realise that the civil unrest was actually a violent protest over the incarceration of the former Malaysian opposition leader Anwar Ibrahim. The extent of the clashes was not fully reported in the Malaysian media. As a result, I was somewhat taken aback the next day when I spoke to my mum on the telephone and she asked me whether I had been near any of the rioting in Kuala Lumpur. Thinking that the Australian media had got a bit carried away in their reporting of the after-hours activities of the athletes, I replied rather defensively that it was hardly a riot — just a couple of us having a few celebratory chardonnays and playing some loud music after our win. Needless to say, Mum was less than impressed with my grasp of current affairs!

Not all of the highlights of my career have been played out in front of television cameras or cheering crowds. A few years ago, I received a copy of a letter that had been sent to Netball Australia by an 'old digger' from Western Australia named Blue Matthews. In it, he complimented the Australian Netball Team on our singing of the national anthem before a test match we had played against New Zealand some days previously. Mr Matthews said: 'As an old digger, I felt ten feet tall, so please from me could you pass this on to those great players, as it helps to lift this great nation up where it belongs.' This letter gave me a bit of a lump in my throat and a tear in my eye. It brought home to me what a privilege it is to represent Australia. It also made me realise that no matter what happens on the court, we must wear our uniform with pride and behave in a manner that makes the people who are sitting at home watching us — from the nine year old who has just pulled on a netball skirt for the first time to the digger who fought for Australia — feel proud that we are their representatives.

So for me, just running onto the court for Australia is a highlight. I get goosebumps every time I sing the national anthem. No matter how many times I do these things, I think I will always get that thrill, regardless of the outcome of the game.

Another off-court highlight was when I was named vice-captain of the Australian team at the beginning of 2000. Kath Harby, Sharon Finnan and myself all put our hands up for one of the top jobs. After submitting our credentials in a written application, and sitting through an interview with

Aussie coach Jill McIntosh and National Executive Director Pam Smith, Kath was named captain and I was chosen as her deputy. While I would dearly have loved to have been named captain, it is an enormous thrill to be part of the leadership team charged with taking Australian netball into the new millennium. I can quite confidently say that Australia was the dominant force in international netball in the nineties. The job has now been given to Kath Harby and myself to ensure that this dominance continues.

With the retirement of Vicki Wilson, Shelley O'Donnell, Carissa Tombs, Jenny Borlase, Simone McKinnis and Nicole Cusack in 1998 and 1999, Kath's and my job was going to be daunting. Just how daunting was proved in June 2000, when Australia was scheduled to meet the Silver Ferns in our first test match since the World Championship final of 1999. The New Zealand team had changed very little, other than the notable addition of former South African shooting superstar Irene van Dyk. On the other hand, our line-up had changed considerably. We had lost an enormous amount of experience over the previous two years, and even though the new line-up boasted some precocious talent, I must admit, I felt a little nervous going into the match.

Any test match is a big occasion, but this game was regarded as a replay of the World Championships final. When the game is also a test of your part in a new leadership team, well, the big occasion becomes an enormous one! As it turned out, I needn't have worried. The new line-up proved that Australia still has the depth of talent to remain on top of the netball world. Despite a shaky start, we ran away with the match, posting a 53–30 win.

It was a great start to a new era of Australian netball.

Chapter 4

Off the Court

Netball is a vital part of my life, but it isn't the only part. Long before I began my international career, I came to the realisation that my chosen sport was not going to pay the bills. Although netball is no longer regarded as a purely amateur sport, it still doesn't generate enough money to pay its representative players. In that respect, netballers are the dinosaurs of sport — we still get out there and play purely for the love of it. Some players are beginning to receive financial assistance from their clubs, although not to the same extent as our footballing or cricketing counterparts. I look forward to the day when top netball players receive financial compensation commensurate with the amount of sacrifice and hard work it takes to be an elite athlete. Unfortunately, I don't think this will happen during my career. Which means, of course, that to pay the bills I had to find something else to do with my time other than play netball.

When I was in Year Twelve, I read a book about a lawyer who was a public prosecutor and it all sounded very interesting and glamorous, so I decided that I would study law at university. After a Higher School Certificate year that was dominated by a lot of netball and almost as much study, I achieved a Tertiary Entrance Rank sufficient for me to enrol in a combined Arts/Law degree at the Australian National University in Canberra.

The main thing that I learned from my decision to try to gain the marks required to study law was to not listen to anyone who told me that I could not achieve what I wanted. I loved playing netball, and I was not going to put it aside for a year to concentrate solely on my studies. So many people told me that I could not successfully do both, as they each took up an inordinate amount of time. Most of the advice I received was to forgo my sport. What appalling advice! Fortunately, my parents encouraged me to do whatever made me happy. They had never put pressure on me to succeed either in netball or at school. Rather, they were there to offer advice when I needed it and to help me achieve my goals. They both expressed a desire that I do well at school with a view to going to university, but had I decided that study was not for me, I have little doubt that they would have supported that decision.

As it turned out, I managed to juggle both. In hindsight, I think that netball and studying complemented rather than detracted from each other. Netball training gave me a break from hours of study, and it refreshed me physically and mentally, enabling me to hit the books well into the night. Netball also gave me an emotional outlet for the stress of the HSC. What better way to take out the frustrations of a day concentrating on maths, physics and history than to run, jump and throw yourself into a standstill. Conversely, applying myself to my study helped the mental side of my netball. As a result, I have never had much trouble focusing on the task at hand in training or during a game. The discipline of concentrating for hours on end at school and university has ultimately been of great benefit to me in my sport.

The six years of study required to complete my degree were not all smooth sailing, so I was pretty happy to finish! I really struggled sometimes to complete assignments in between training weekends and tours, and I missed a lot of classes due to netball commitments. It was certainly worth it though, and I was really proud to graduate with a Bachelor of Arts combined with a Bachelor of Laws.

I was also really excited about being admitted to the Supreme Court in 1998. After six years of university and four months training at the College of Law, it was a really proud moment for me and my family.

Since my admission, I have practised as a solicitor with top-tier firm Corrs Chambers Westgarth. Fortunately, they are incredibly supportive of my netball career, and I never have any problems getting time off to train or compete — although one of my colleagues recently suggested that I should fill in leave forms for the days I would actually be in the office, rather than for the days I'm away. I must admit, I am the only solicitor in the firm with my own pad of leave forms!

I have also been incredibly fortunate to pick up some great sponsors who are associated with me through the Liz Ellis Coaching Clinics. My associations with Nike, Kellogg's Corn Flakes, Reliance Netballs, 2KY and Horsell Insurance have allowed me to pursue my dreams without having to worry about where my next meal is coming from.

One difficult thing for me to come to terms with is the struggle netballers have to receive recognition for our achievements on the court. Certainly, there have been enormous improvements over the last ten years, but I believe netball has a long way to go before its elite players are given adequate recognition. Netball fans often tell me how disappointed they are at the lack of coverage the sport receives in mainstream media outlets. My answer to that is, don't tell me — tell the people who make those decisions! Newspaper editors and television and radio producers need to be made aware that they are not catering to the interests of a portion of their audience. By not giving women's sport similar coverage to men's, they are effectively alienating half the market. By the same token, these people should be congratulated when they get it right.

This struggle for media recognition is not limited to netball. Many female athletes face this dilemma. Nothing makes me happier than to see athletic women held up as strong, positive role models for young girls to look up to and emulate. It doesn't matter what sport they play — hockey, basketball, cricket or netball, or whether they run, swim, jump, ride horses or hit tennis balls – elite female athletes deserve to be recognised for their contribution to Australian sport.

I believe that as athletes we have a responsibility to be positive role models for women, both young and mature. This belief was the reasoning behind the Aussie Netball Team's decision not to pose naked for our 2001 calendar. In a team meeting, we decided that posing naked wasn't part of the image we would like to portray. There have been some sporting teams in the past who have done this, but we felt that as a team, we had a responsibility to our fans to maintain the positive image that we had worked so hard for. In our minds, we wanted to be recognised for our achievements as a team representing our country, so it was a reasonably easy decision for us to make.

Even with the benefit of hindsight, I believe we made the right decision. At times, it has been tempting to grab some headlines and force our way into the limelight with pictures of our scantily clad team, but at the end of the day, I would prefer to grab those headlines because of our spectacular achievements on the court. Getting this media exposure isn't going to be easy, but given the number of netball fans in Australia, I believe it is an achievable dream.

Chapter 5

Coaching

I decided several years ago that I would like to give something back to netball. I really enjoy coaching and I would love to be able to take a young team through a netball season. Time — or lack thereof — precludes me from doing this. Instead, I run day-long coaching clinics for young players.

I began holding netball coaching clinics in 1997. In the first year, about 300 young players attended six clinics, which I held in conjunction with various associations. Four years later, the number of clinics I hold has grown to sixteen per year with almost 2000 players attending. I get an awful lot of pleasure from meeting these young players and seeing them improve their skills throughout the day. Their eyes really light up when they master a skill or learn something new. I must admit that watching it makes my eyes light up as well!

My basic coaching philosophy is that netball should be fun. As players move through the ranks and improve in ability, there are different ways for the coach to ensure that their players are enjoying themselves. When coaching netta players, I try to ensure that the drills are fun but have an underlying purpose of developing the players' basic motor skills. For the older age groups, I believe that the fun should come from acquiring a new skill, although I find that, regardless of the age group, all players enjoy a fun game or drill at the conclusion of the session. There are plenty of resources available about coaching using fun games for both netta and older players. To access these resources just contact your state netball association.

I like to break sessions up into four fifteen to twenty minute blocks (excluding warm-up) in order to replicate a game situation. Using this schedule in training gets players used to working hard for the period of time a match runs, and it also trains players to concentrate for the full length of the match.

I am a great believer in making the blocks of training sessions specific. For example, the first block may be a ball-work circuit or pairs, the second block working on team passing and timing drills, the third could be attacking and defensive work, and the fourth working on long-court systems or playing a half-court game. Time should also be spent working on specific tactics for upcoming matches.

I think it is particularly important that drills are not done just for the sake of it. Drills should have a specific objective. As a player, I have always worked better in drills when the coach has taken the time to explain their purpose. The objective of a particular drill may be simple, such as getting the players to catch hard passes, or more complicated, such as working on double plays or driving along the baseline.

I enjoy drills that start simply and then have different components added until they begin to resemble on-court situations. These sorts of 'progressive' drills allow players to work on one particular thing at a time and then transfer what they've learnt to a game-like situation. Hopefully, the player will then be able to reproduce her new skill the next time she plays netball.

It is also necessary for players to practise executing different skills when they are fatigued. It is all very well for players to be able to catch safely, steady their feet and pass strongly at the beginning of the session when they are feeling fresh. It is another thing to still have these skills at the end of a tight game when the body is screaming out to sit down and have a rest. To this end, the coach needs to ensure that players work at full capacity all the way through the training session so that they become used to producing skilful work even when they are tired.

From a player's point of view, this is important as well. A season is a long time to spend turning up to training week after week and practising netball skills. Players need to be challenged to work hard while they are there. I like turning up to training and absolutely working myself to a standstill. Turning up and standing around talking is a waste of time — if you have to be at training you might as well get something good out of it.

Most of the following chapters are based upon the skills I teach at the Liz Ellis Netball Clinics. I hope that they will help you not only to improve your netball, but also to get greater enjoyment out of the game by expanding your repertoire of skills.

Chapter 6

Warm-up

Before undertaking any form of training it is necessary to warm up properly. A good warm-up serves two important purposes. Firstly, it readies your body for action by preparing the muscles for the workout ahead. Running and stretching increase the blood flow to your soft tissue, which in turn allows you to perform the explosive movements required for a netball game or training session. Secondly, it helps to prevent injury. Getting the soft tissue warm will help to prevent muscle tears as well as tendon and ligament strains.

A good warm-up should begin at a low intensity with general exercises (such as light running) and build up to specific exercises and drills performed at high intensity. Warm-ups should be intense enough to make you start to sweat but not so intense that you start to feel tired.

I find that the older I get, the more warm-up I need! I have some vague memories of being able to turn up to a netball game and run onto the court after passing the ball around for about five minutes. These memories are vague for good reason — they are from days long past! Now I find it necessary to perform a good thirty minutes of warm-up exercises before a game. Competing in elite competition, whether it be the Commonwealth Bank Trophy or a test match, means that I need to be ready to go at 100 per cent from the moment I step onto the court — there is no time to use the first couple of minutes of the game as warm-up. If I did that, not only would I risk injury, but I would also be given the run around by my opponent!

When I first started playing representative netball, our pre-match warm-up consisted of running six to eight laps of the court, about ten minutes of stretching, and finished with some sprints down the court and some dodging and jumping.

The way we approach our warm-up exercises has changed somewhat over the last few years. New research suggests that less stretching and more general movement is a better preparation than the old jog, stretch, sprint routine. As a result, both the Swifts and the Australian team have made significant changes to the way we get our bodies ready to play.

Ideally, a warm-up should start a couple of hours before the game. Don't worry — you won't need to be running or jumping around during this time! Rather, the pre-warm-up routine involves stretching for twenty to thirty minutes. These stretches act as a 'pre-warning' to the muscles that you are about to do some exercise and they had better get themselves ready. We started this practice at the 1999 World Championships. Basically, we went through our normal stretching routine about forty-five minutes before we were due to board the bus to the courts. It was an incredibly beneficial thing to do. When we used to warm up without stretching a couple of hours beforehand, I was often quite stiff for the first couple of laps of our initial warm-up jog. Once I started stretching beforehand, I felt ready from the moment we started to run.

The stretching routine includes all of the major muscle groups. I also pay special attention to my back. I have a chronic back injury, which I keep under control by working on flexibility and abdominal strength. I am certainly not the most flexible person in the world — I am the least flexible player on the Australian team. On a good day, I can touch my toes, and on a bad day it hurts just to stretch my imagination! Nevertheless, I do try to keep some flexibility in my muscles and this is why the pre-warm-up stretching routine is so important.

Stretching

Generally, I start off by stretching my groin, then my hamstrings, gluteus maximus (a fancy word for bum), lower back, hip flexor, calves, quadriceps (or thighs) and arms. There are several stretches that can be done for each of these areas.

Groin/Adductor

Sit on the ground with your knees bent away from your body and put the soles of your feet together. Hold on to your ankles and place your elbows on your knees. Gently push your knees towards the ground.

Hamstrings

Sit on the ground with one leg lying flat out in front of you. Place the sole of the other foot so that it is touching the knee of your straight leg. Keeping your back straight, bend forward from the hips and try to touch the toes of your straight leg.

Gluteus maximus/Lower back

Sit on the ground with one leg lying flat out in front of you. Bend your other leg and place your foot flat on the ground on the outside of your straight knee. Grab the crossed leg, using the forearm of the opposite arm. If, for example, it is your right leg, pull it towards your left shoulder with your left arm. To increase the stretch, turn and look over your other shoulder.

Lower back

Lie on your back with both knees bent at 90° angles so that your feet are flat on the ground. Keeping your bent knees together, slowly lower them to one side, keeping your shoulders on the ground. Repeat on the other side.

Hip flexor

The hip flexor is an important muscle to concentrate on when you are stretching. If this muscle is tight, it tends to put pressure on your back, which can lead to a lower back injury. To stretch the hip flexor, you kneel down on one knee. Place the foot of your other leg flat on the ground in front of you, making sure you keep your shin and thigh at a 90° angle. Gently lean forward, transferring your weight from the knee of your back leg to the foot of your front leg until you can feel the stretch down the front of the back leg.

Calves

Find a step and stand on it. Put one foot on the next step up for balance. Move your back foot so that the ball of your foot is at the edge of the step and gently drop your heel over the edge. To stretch the bottom of the calf, bend your back leg slightly. To stretch the rest of the muscle, keep your back leg straight.

Quadriceps

To stretch your right quad, balance on your left leg, grab hold of your right ankle with your right hand and gently pull the heel towards your right buttock. To increase the stretch, push your hips forward. Repeat for your left quad. To prevent overbalancing while doing this stretch, you can either lean against something (or someone!), focus on a point on the ground, put the index finger of your free hand in your belly button, or hold onto your earlobe with your free hand.

Biceps

Stand next to a wall. Reach the arm closest to the wall straight out beside you and place your palm on the wall at shoulder height. To stretch your right bicep, gently turn to your left until you feel the stretch in your bicep. To stretch your left bicep, do the same but turn to your right. This stretch can also be done using a netball post by gently holding onto the post with your hand at shoulder level.

Triceps

Lift your arm up so that it is parallel with the ground. Place your other hand on the outside of your elbow and pull it towards your body.

Forearms

Hold one arm out straight with the palm facing up. With the other hand, gently push the fingers of the outstretched hand towards the ground.

Fingers

Steeple your fingertips and gently push your fingers against each other.

These are just some examples of stretches that can be performed on the major muscle groups. Ideally, each muscle should be stretched twice in order to get maximum flexibility.

As a general rule, stretches should be held for a minimum of twenty seconds each. Also, you should stretch so far as to cause tension in the targeted muscle, but not so much as to cause pain. Over-stretching may cause microscopic tears in the muscle, which can lead to scar tissue forming in your muscles. This scar tissue can mean a loss of elasticity and flexibility.

When you arrive at the netball courts, it is necessary to perform a full warm-up, which, as I said earlier, takes about thirty minutes. With the Swifts, we start off by jogging up and down the court for three to five minutes, which raises our heart rate. This is followed by two or three minutes of stretching (which we all try to extend because it feels so good!).

The current trend is to spend less time standing still and stretching for a warm-up, as one of the effects of this kind of stretching may be to actually relax the muscles rather than prepare them for a hard game of netball! The warm-up should consist of a short jog to warm the muscles followed by some dynamic stretching. Old habits die hard though, and we were reluctant to completely discard the static stretching.

Following the static stretching, we jog for a couple of minutes and then go into some dynamic stretching, which stretches the muscles while they are moving. We use the following dynamic stretches.

Sidestep

Place feet shoulder-width apart and balance on the balls of your feet. With short, sharp movements take small sideways steps. Be careful not to drag your feet along the ground or kick your feet together in the middle of the step. Sidestep down one length of the court, turning 180° to face the other sideline halfway down the court.

Bodyweight squat

Put your hands out in front of your body and bend your knees to 90°, keeping your feet flat on the ground. As far as possible, try to keep your knees directly above your ankles. Do ten of these.

Running backwards

Run backwards for one length of the court.

Tuck jumps

Jump as high as you can and tuck your feet up under your body. Do five of these.

Skipping

Skip for one length of the court, skipping as high as you can every third step.

Leg swings

Lean sideways against a wall and swing each leg back and forwards, then face the wall and swing each leg from side to side. Do this five times in each direction for each leg. Try to keep your shoulders, trunk and hips in a straight line.

Grapevine

This is similar to a sidestep, except that instead of stepping crab-like to the side, the left foot crosses in front of the right foot, the right foot then steps right and the left foot crosses behind the right foot. Do this for one length of the court, turning 180° to face the other sideline halfway down.

Push ups

Start doing push-ups with your knees and try to progress to only having your toes on the ground as you get stronger. Do ten of these.

Running left and right

Take two to three steps diagonally left and push off your left foot, then two steps diagonally right and push off your right foot. Do this for one length of the court.

Side lunges

Start with both feet together. Lunge out to the left with one wide step so that you can feel the stretch in your adductors (the inside of the thighs), then bring the left foot back to the middle. Do the same with the right leg. Do this five times with each leg.

High knees

Over the length of a third, take as many small steps as possible while lifting your knees as high as you can.

Bum kicks

Take lots of small steps over the same distance as you did for the high knees, while kicking your bum (gently!) with your heels.

Split squats

Place one foot out in front and squat down so that your front leg is bent at 90° at the knee, and the knee of the back leg almost touches the ground. Do this five times on each leg. You should feel the stretch down the front of your back leg.

These are just some examples of dynamic stretching. Some players do more than this, and some do less, depending on the needs of their bodies. This warm-up can be tailored to a particular team or player by making up your own movements. The Sydney Swifts came up with this routine after trying different things for a couple of months in our pre-season. The only rule for dynamic stretching is that there should be at least one movement for each major muscle group. Other movements may be ankle hops, running while touching the ground every five metres on alternate sides, arm swings, single leg hops and alternate toe touches, just to name a few.

Once the dynamic warm-up has been completed, my team-mates and I take a couple of minutes to complete our stretching, or to re-stretch any muscles that feel as if they need some extra attention.

After completing my stretching routine, I am ready to carry out some court sprints at 100 per cent. These sprints are pretty simple. Generally, they consist of a couple of run throughs — which means I jog the first third, sprint through the middle third and jog the last third — as well as some sprints off the mark.

After the sprints, it is time to move on to some ball work. With both the Swifts and the Australian team, we start doing ball work in pairs. Many players have their own routine for 'pairs' and it is simply a matter of each individual finding what works for them. I prefer to do several activities that intersperse movement with stationary work. Some players prefer to do less — I was always amazed at the capacity of Carissa Tombs to perform a predominantly stationary pairs routine and then come out and blast away her opponents with her speed and power. Perhaps she was just being smart and conserving her energy until it counted!

The routine that Alison Williams and I perform before a Sydney Swifts game is fairly simple. We start off about a metre apart and, while running on the spot (called pitter-pattering), we flick the ball to each other using only our fingers for about ten passes each. We then move further apart and one works while the other throws chest passes to her. The worker pitter-patters and takes one step forward to catch the ball, keeping her back foot on the ground. We generally do three of these on each foot. We then repeat the process, but this time stepping out to the side. The next movement is for the worker to start on a pitter-patter and run towards the thrower, receiving a variety of passes. When we catch the ball, we pass it back to the thrower and run backwards to our starting point, pitter-patter and go again.

The next part of the routine is stationary, where we do about ten 'hooks' each. To perform a 'hook', two players stand about one metre away from each other. The worker starts with her hands resting comfortably on her thighs. The thrower tosses the ball gently in the air, about an arm's length from the worker's body. The worker quickly reaches out with her left or right arm, depending which is closest to the ball. When the worker gets her hand on the ball, she 'hooks' it back in towards her body as fast as she can, bringing the other hand up quickly to get both hands on the ball and ensure ball security. The worker then returns the ball to the thrower. We do about ten of these each.

Finally, we finish off with a movement which involves the worker running to her left and taking a chest pass, then to her right and taking a chest pass, then running to the thrower and picking up a ball that the thrower drops at her feet. It ends with the worker running backwards to take a lob. The worker then comes back to her starting point and repeats the series of movements.

While this is a pretty busy warm-up routine, Ali and I actually get quite a lot of rest time when we are the thrower in each drill.

The final phase of our warm-up is to carry out some team drills. As a general rule, both the Australian team and the Sydney Swifts have three set drills for this particular phase. The first drill usually includes some form of reaction, whereby a thrower throws the ball in a way that makes the worker chase it down. The drill also includes an element of timing, so that we can get into a rhythm with our team-mates.

The first team drill that the Swifts and the Australian team do is a good example of a reaction drill. The key to this drill is to keep it short. The players start off in four even lines, making up a small square of about three metres by three metres (as shown in Figure 6.1 by the lines marked A, B, C and D). Two players start with a ball each at T1 and T2 and throw a 'reaction' pass to the player opposite them (W1 and W2 in the figure). W1 and W2 run towards their respective thrower to collect the ball. W1 passes back to T1 and W2 back to T2. The thrower then throws another reaction pass. The worker catches it, turns and passes to

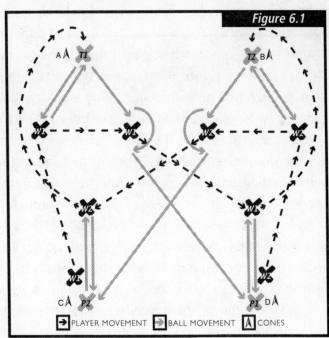

Figure 6.1

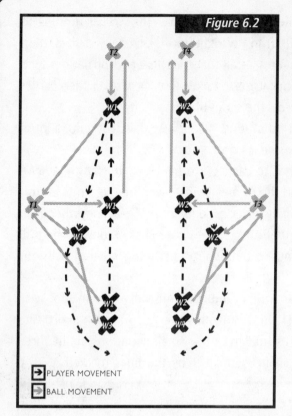

Figure 6.2

PLAYER MOVEMENT

BALL MOVEMENT

the first player in line diagonally opposite her. (So, in the figure, W1 will pass to P1 and W2 to P2.) W1 then drives towards P1, and W2 towards P2. W1 receives a straight pass from P1, and W2 from P2. W1 then throws the ball back to P1 and runs behind line B, and W2 throws back to P2 and runs behind line A. The drill then starts again, this time from the opposite end.

I really like this drill for two reasons. Firstly, there is plenty of movement, so it gets me going physically. Secondly, it is a drill that makes me think, so I find it helps to get me focused for the game ahead.

After this, we do another short drill. Place four throwers (T1, T2, T3 and T4) as shown in Figure 6.2. Line up the rest of the players as workers as shown. (Each line works independently and identically at first, so I will just describe what one line does until they intersect.) W1 starts with the ball and throws a straight pass to T1 and runs to receive a chest pass back from T1. W1 then throws the ball to T2 and runs straight towards her to receive a short reaction pass. W1 then throws the ball to T1 then runs back towards the worker's line and receives another pass from T1. W1 offloads the ball to the next worker in her line, W3. Once the players have been through the drill twice, they move on to the second phase. In this phase, when W1 receives the reaction pass from T2 she passes it to T4 on the opposite side, instead of T1. She receives her next pass from T4 and offloads the ball to the worker at the top of the opposite line to the one she started in. She then joins the back of this line.

After a short rest, we finish our warm-up with a longer timing drill that usually takes up half of the court. We try to change the timing drill each year so we don't get bored with doing the same thing. Essentially, the timing drill should include a variety of passes such as shoulder passes, chest passes and lobs, and movements such as jumping, dodging and sprinting.

Finally, there should always be time in a pre-match warm-up for the goalers to practise their goals and get their eye in. The warm-up should not be rushed, and there should be sufficient time before the game starts for players to rest and rehydrate without cooling down.

If you are participating in a carnival that involves playing several games throughout the day, it won't be necessary for you to perform a full warm-up before each game. If you only have a twenty to thirty minute break between games, your body will not cool down completely. Try and fit in a couple of minutes of stretching during the break between games, and then spend at least five minutes doing some low-intensity ball work, moving to high intensity. To save time, try jogging from your rest area to your court as part of your warm-up.

Top Tips

1. *The warm-up should be something that your team works on in the pre-season. By the time the season starts your team should be able to do your warm-up blindfolded. If you know your warm-up well, it will help you to prepare for the game mentally as well as physically. This is because the warm-up is a routine that should make you feel comfortable for the game ahead.*

2. *To prevent you from getting bored with your warm-up, your team can develop two or three different warm-up routines and use them on alternate weeks.*

3. *Make sure that you drink plenty of fluid during your warm-up so that you are not dehydrated when you take the court.*

Chapter 7

Basic Skills

I cannot emphasise enough the importance of every young netball player developing basic skills. From the moment you step onto a netball court, you need to receive instruction in the basics of passing, catching and footwork.

Essentially, netball is a very simple game. The ball must travel from one end of the court to the other by way of players passing the ball to each other for the goalers to attempt a goal. There is very little point in developing complicated tactics, or in training players for endurance and speed, if they do not have a good grasp of the fundamentals of the game. All top-level netball players base their games on the fundamental aspects of the sport. There would be no use in players like Sharelle McMahon and Catherine Cox practising their goal shooting if they were unable to catch the ball in the first place. There would be little point in Kath Harby, Janine Ilitch or Liz Taverner anticipating a spectacular defensive intercept if they couldn't move their feet to get them there. And Rebecca Sanders would have very little use for her speed if she could not deliver a good feed into the circle. Fortunately, all of these players have mastered the basic skills of netball, which form the basis of the special things they do on court.

Even in the Australian team we still focus on our basic skills at the start of a training session. Basic skills are things that need to be worked on in order to become adept at them, and then touched on regularly after that.

Catching

Catching is the most important of the basic skills. There is no use learning passing and footwork if the player is not capable of catching the ball. Despite its importance, the art of catching is reasonably simple. The player holds her hands so that her thumbs are almost touching and her fingers are out to the side. The fingers should not be tense but nice and relaxed so that they can grasp the ball. If the fingers are pointing straight forwards there is the risk that the ball will injure the player by jarring her fingers. If the fingers are pointing straight out to the side then the player won't be able to grasp the ball as it reaches her hands.

However, merely catching the ball as it comes to you is not enough. There are often situations in the game where a player is required to catch the ball under considerable pressure from an opponent. At these times, it is necessary not only to be able to catch the ball, but also to pull it in aggressively. One of the most aggressive players onto the ball is Sharelle McMahon. If you watch her carefully, you will see that there are many times during a game when her defender is in front of her and looks like getting an intercept, only for Sharelle to take an extra step onto the ball and snatch it in with both hands. I know that whenever I come up against her, I have to be prepared to run hard at the ball if I am to have a chance of getting it.

Players can practise snatching the ball in aggressively. Essentially, it is a matter of the player getting two hands on the ball and pulling it in to her chest so that it is protected. To do this drill, one player (the worker) stands one metre away from the player with the ball (the thrower) with her hands resting on her thighs. The thrower tosses the ball gently towards the worker and the worker reacts as quickly as she can to the throw, pulling the ball to her chest the moment she gets her hands on it. As the worker's reaction time becomes faster, the thrower can start to vary the direction and height of the ball toss, including dropping it to the ground. The hardest to catch, and the final step in the drill, is the 'hook', which is when the ball is put at the very limit of the worker's reach, and she 'hooks' it in with one hand so that she can get her other hand on it. These drills are useful as part of a pre-match warm-up. I really enjoy doing them because they not only get my hands working but also help me tune in for the game.

Another good drill is to have a thrower standing on a transverse line with the worker standing opposite her on the other transverse line. The worker starts by moving her feet in a 'pitter-patter' motion and then sprints towards the thrower. After the worker takes her first few steps, the thrower passes a shoulder pass to the worker. Not only does the worker have to pull that ball in with both hands, but she must also continue to run forward until the ball is safely in her hands. The aim of this drill is to get players used to running onto the ball, rather than standing and waiting until the ball reaches them. This drill is particularly important for attack players because, defensively, it is much easier to get an intercept when the ball is thrown to a stationary player rather than a moving one.

Once the worker has caught the ball, she passes it back to the thrower, runs backwards to the line and goes again. This should be done approximately five or six times. The next step is for the thrower to pass a bounce pass, then a lob and eventually for the thrower to pass a variety of passes for the worker to react to. This particular drill is something that Alison Williams and I do religiously as part of our pre-match warm-up with the Sydney Swifts.

Passing

There are five passes that are commonly used in a game of netball. These are: chest, shoulder, bounce, overhead passes and lobs. Each pass has a specific purpose, and a player's pass selection depends upon the situation in which she finds herself. As a defender whose job it is to get the ball away from the opposition's goal post as fast as possible, I tend to choose these simple, safe passes.

On the other hand, an attacking player needs to develop a greater repertoire of passes in order to create opportunities to score. Former New Zealand captain and magical centre-court player Sandra Edge possessed a wicked look-away pass. She would look one way and throw the other, and as a defender, there is nothing harder to pick. Nicole Cusack had a similar move — not only would she look one way and pass the other, but she would also fake her body to move one way and flick the ball in the opposite direction. Vicki Wilson used to pride herself on being able to throw equally as well with her left hand as with her right, while Shelley O'Donnell has the ability to move even the best defences with a clever baulk in order to clear the way for a pass to her goalers.

Each of these skills can be developed with much practise, although to perform them at an elite level demands a fair degree of cunning! And while these passes look tricky, they are the result of proficiency in basic passes.

Passing well requires the player to have a certain familiarity with the ball. Players need to know what the ball feels like in their hands in order for them to successfully execute each of the passes. This can be achieved through individual ball work at the beginning of a session. It is also something that players can do in their own time to develop an affinity with the feel of the ball.

As the idea behind individual ball work is to establish a familiarity with the feel of the ball, most of the drills set out below should be done without the player looking at the ball.

Individual Ball Drills

Drill One

Move the ball from hand to hand around your head, waist and knees. Keeping your eyes off the ball, do this five to ten times clockwise then repeat anticlockwise. Focus on keeping the ball on your fingertips and maintaining control of the ball around your body in a spiralling motion.

Drill Two

Stand with your feet apart and hold the ball in front of your knees. Bounce the ball between your feet then move your hands behind your knees and catch the ball. Do this five to ten times while keeping your eyes up.

The aim of this drill is to control the ball on release and to increase the speed of your hand movements. Once you've perfected this drill, you can toss the ball and catch it behind your knees without letting the ball bounce.

Drill Three

Stand with your feet apart and your knees bent. Hold the ball between your knees with one hand in front of your knees and the other hand behind your knees. Let the ball bounce and swing your hands around so that the front hand moves behind your knees and the back hand moves to the front to catch the ball before it bounces a second time. Do this five to ten times while keeping your eyes up.

This drill will increase the speed of your hand movements. Once you can do this drill successfully, try tossing the ball and catching it without letting it bounce.

Drill Four

Stand with your feet apart and move the ball around and through your knees in a figure eight. Do this five to ten times and keep your eyes up.

This drill will help perfect your control of the ball. Once you can do this, try reversing the movement so that the ball moves from the back of your body to the front instead.

Drill Five

Hold the ball behind your head at the top of your neck. Let go of the ball so that it rolls down your back. Quickly move your hands so that they are outstretched behind you with your thumbs facing each other and with your palms up. Catch the ball. Do this five to ten times.

This drill will not only increase the speed of your hand movements but will also help you to control the ball once you feel it in your hands. Once you have mastered this drill, start with the ball in front of you and toss it over your head. Then move your hands behind your back to catch the ball.

Drill Six

Begin by holding the ball in front of you. Toss it into the air and clap once before catching it. The next time, you toss it up, clap twice; the next time three times and so on until you can clap ten times.

This drill will help you to control the toss of the ball. Make sure your hands are strong on the catch. This means getting a strong grip on the ball and pulling it in to your body. Once you have perfected this, try clapping in front and behind your body.

Drill Seven

Begin by holding the ball in front of you. Throw the ball into the air and touch the ground before you catch it.

Once you are proficient at this, you toss the ball up and turn 360° before catching the ball. Do each of these five to ten times.

Make sure you have strong hands on the catch. When you can do each of these movements, combine them by throwing the ball up, turning around and touching the ground before catching the ball.

Top Tips

Individual ball skills can also be practised against a wall.

Start about one metre away from the wall, holding the ball in your left hand. Tap the ball against the wall, controlling it with your fingertips.

Still tapping, slowly move up the wall until the ball is above your head. When the ball is above your head, change to your right hand without stopping. Move the ball slowly down the wall and then back up again until it is above your head. Change back to your left hand.

If you are really clever, try this with your eyes closed!

Just a couple of important points about passing before I get into the specifics of the different passes.

Firstly, it is absolutely vital that you learn from an early age to step forward as you throw. Whenever you pass the ball, you should step forward onto your left foot if you are right-handed, or onto your right foot if you are left-handed. This movement will give you the necessary balance to execute a pass, and also provides the requisite power to drill a pass to the intended recipient. This is particularly important for a shoulder pass, where it is difficult to throw the ball a reasonable distance and at a reasonable speed without the initial forward movement of the feet.

Secondly, it is imperative that you understand that your fingers will dictate where the ball is going to go. For example, if you throw a shoulder pass and your fingers finish the follow-through pointing at the ground, I would expect that is exactly where the ball will finish up — on the ground. When going through the basic passes, either in warm-up or as a part of the training session, you should concentrate on exaggerating the follow-through to ensure that your fingers are pointing in the right direction.

Chest Pass

To execute a chest pass, stand with your feet approximately shoulder-width apart, with both of your hands on the ball, with your fingers facing forwards. Lift the ball to your chest with your hands on either side of the ball, and in doing so rotate your hands slightly so that your fingers are pointing upwards. As you step forward to throw, move your fingers to push the ball away from you and into the pass.

On release, both arms should be out in front of the body, with the fingers pointing in the direction of the chest of the player receiving the ball. It is important that you do not favour one hand over the other when passing a chest pass. If, for example, you favour your left hand when executing a chest pass, it is likely that the ball will skew off to your right.

Shoulder Pass

Stand as you would for a chest pass, holding the ball with both hands in front of you. Lift the ball to a position just outside your right shoulder (if you are right-handed), so that your fingers and thumb are making a 'V' behind the ball. The ball should be held primarily in the fingers, rather than in the palm of your hand. As you step forward to throw, drop your left hand and pass the ball with your right hand only. Again, the fingers of your throwing arm should be extended in the direction the pass is intended to go.

The most common mistake I see when conducting my clinics is players forgetting to drop their other hand away from the ball before they pass. This results in an inferior pass: a two-handed shoulder pass lacks the power and accuracy of its one-handed sister.

Shoulder passes can also get a bit loopy — in the nicest possible way! If this happens, check the fingers of the throwing arm prior to release. Players who throw loopy shoulder passes will often do so because their fingers are pointing directly up and their thumb is pointing towards their ear. The result of holding the ball like this, is that as the fingers move forward they flick the ball into the air, making the pass appear more like a lob than a shoulder pass.

Bounce Pass

Personally, I hate bounce passes (as does every defender) as they are harder to intercept than other passes. As a result, they are a handy weapon for an attacking player to possess.

The bounce pass is similar to the shoulder pass in that the player takes the same stance then moves the ball to the side of her body. The requirements of the game situation will dictate exactly where the pass is released from. For example, a bounce pass may be released quite low if you are passing to a goaler holding front space and you don't want the ball to bounce up high enough for the defender to have a go at it. If, on the other hand, you are throwing a bounce pass to get around a taller opponent and you are passing to a player who is moving, you may wish to release the ball higher so that it bounces up to the intended recipient and allows her to move onto the pass.

As a general rule, the bounce pass is released close to your hip area. Take the ball to your side in both hands and, as you step forward, drop your left hand (if you are right-handed or your right hand if you are left-handed) and bounce the ball to the intended recipient with one hand. It is important to aim the ball so that it bounces close enough to the recipient's feet to ensure that it bounces up no higher than the top of her legs. On some occasions it may be necessary to bounce the ball so that it goes no higher than the recipient's knees! The reason for keeping the bounce low is that after it bounces the ball slows down somewhat, so the longer it is in the air after it bounces, the more chance there is of an intercept. Just remember to bounce the ball — don't 'skim' it across the ground.

Lob

The lob is a really useful pass when thrown properly. As a goal keeper, it is also the one that I have to defend against the most in international competition. Most of the goalers from the top nations tower over me, so I reckon I have seen more lobs go over my head than most people have had roast dinners. Despite this, there is some risk in throwing a lob as it is easier to intercept than other passes. Firstly, it spends more time in the air than other passes, so it allows defenders time to move their feet and have a go at the ball. Secondly, the lob pass must be placed well to ensure that it reaches the player it is intended for. If it drops short, it is likely to fall straight into the defender's hands. If it is too long, it will go over the recipient's head.

In the Commonwealth Bank Trophy, it is really only Joanne Morgan from the Sydney Sandpipers who relies heavily on the lob to receive the ball. This is understandable given the fact that she is 190 centimetres tall and able to hold space well. It also means that those players feeding her have to know how to execute the perfect lob!

To throw a lob, stand with your feet shoulder-width apart and hold the ball in front of you with both hands. Like a shoulder pass, lift the ball to a position (if you are right-handed) just outside your right shoulder. However, rather than making your fingers and thumb form a 'V' which faces directly upwards, as you would for a shoulder pass, make the 'V' slightly skewed so that your fingers are pointing upwards and your thumb is pointing towards your head.

If you are right-handed, drop your left hand and, as you step forward, move your throwing hand up and out. When you release the ball, your throwing arm should be at a 45° angle. Ensure that you release the ball at the highest possible point. A lob is usually thrown to get the ball over a tall opponent, so it makes sense to release it as high as possible. At the same time, it is important that you do not release the ball with your hand directly above your head, as the ball will go nowhere other than straight up in the air and down again.

The lob pass requires some input from the intended recipient as well as from you. As it is a high-risk pass, it needs to be thrown with a certain degree of accuracy. For this to happen, the receiver needs to position her body so that you can easily see where her space is. In order to do this, the receiver needs to angle her body so that either her left or right hand is facing away from you. You would then aim to throw the ball to the receiver's back hand. The reason for this is that in a game situation, where the receiver has a defender in front of her, she needs to create some space behind her for the ball to be thrown into. If the receiver sets up facing directly towards the thrower, she is not clearly indicating a space she can move into to receive the ball.

Overhead Pass

Overhead passes aren't as common as the other four passes, and with good reason. They can't be thrown as hard over as long a distance as a shoulder pass, nor are they as accurate as a chest pass. Nevertheless, they are a useful little number to have up your sleeve.

To throw an overhead pass, start with your feet shoulder-width apart and with the ball in both hands. Hold the ball just above your head, so that your elbows are about level with your eyes. Just before you step forward, drop the ball slightly behind your head and, as you take a step, straighten your elbows and move your arms forwards to release the ball. The pass should be straight and reasonably hard, with most of the power coming from your forward movement.

Passing Drill

There is a useful and fun drill that can be varied to incorporate each of these passes. You will need a minimum of ten players to make this drill work. Divide the players into two even teams and line them up down the court with the two lines facing each other. Pair off each player with the one opposite, and give each pair a number as shown in Figure 7.1

Place two balls in the middle of the lines. When the coach calls a number, the players allocated that number run and pick up a ball each. They then run to the end of the line that is furthest away from the goal post and pass the ball to the first player in the line. The player must pass the ball to and receive it back from each player on her team, moving down the line as she passes. When the player gets to the person closest to the circle, the pass she receives from her last team-mate must be close to the post. The player then shoots, rebounding her shot if necessary and shooting again until she gets it in. The first player to get the shot in receives a point for her team.

Figure 7.1

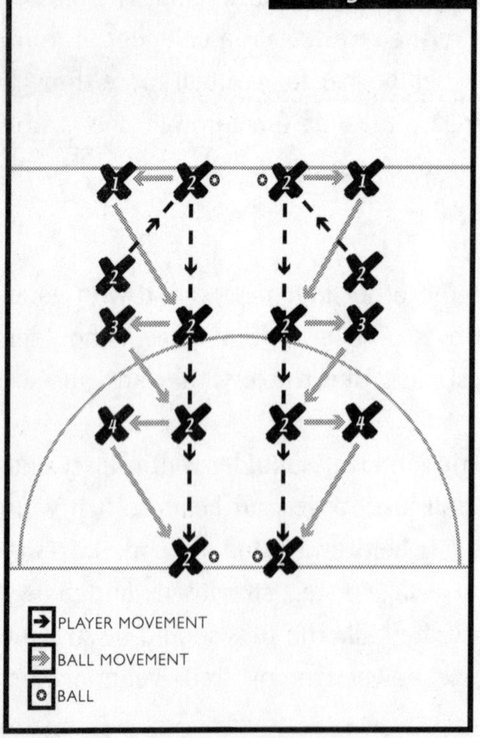

PLAYER MOVEMENT
BALL MOVEMENT
BALL

The reason that this drill is a good one for practising passes is that the coach can vary the passes the player must throw as she moves down the line. The length of the line can also be varied by moving the players further away from each other. More experienced players can be as far away as the sideline and spread out down the full length of the court.

The variations to this drill are limitless, with players' interest maintained by the fact that it is a competition.

Top Tips

1. Practise passing the ball with both hands — you never know when you may need to dispose of the ball with your weaker hand! To do this, you can stand about three metres away from a wall and throw a netball against the wall, first with your right and then with your left hand.

2. Practise throwing all of your passes with both hands until you can do each one reasonably well.

3. Once you can do each of the passes, it is time to work on accuracy. Mark a spot on the wall and practise hitting that spot twenty times, using each hand.

4. Next, start facing away from the wall and toss the ball above your head. As you catch the ball, pivot to face the wall, spot the mark and throw the ball at the mark.

5. Finally, start about five metres away from the wall, toss the ball in the air, turn, spot the mark and pass the ball to the mark. The moment you release the ball, sprint towards the wall and catch the ball as it rebounds.

Ball-work circuit

Many basic ball skills can be practised at the start of the training session with a ball-work circuit. This is a great way to start training as it warms the players up, provides some specific netball fitness, and gives players the opportunity to work on their basic ball-work skills when they are fatigued after carrying out each movement section of the circuit. As a general rule, make the work high intensity and allow plenty of rest time. This can be achieved by splitting the group into pairs with one ball between them. The circuit should include basic ball skills combined with plenty of running. I also use lots of cones! The best sort are soft plastic ones that collapse when you stand on them.

The way I structure my circuit is to have at least one activity per pair. If you have ten players, this means that there are five activity stations to be worked at for three minutes each. If there are only three or four pairs, you should still have at least five stations, as three minutes is long enough to spend on one activity. At each station I have a movement drill along with a stationary ball-work drill, so that the players do not move on to the next station until they have completed the movement phase and the stationary phase. If there are more than ten players, you can add a station for each extra pair in the group and just reduce the amount of time spent at each station.

Assuming there are five pairs, here is an example of a fifteen-minute ball-work circuit.

Station One

Movement: Set up four cones in a square about a metre and a half apart. The thrower, standing outside the square, throws reaction passes to the worker, who works within the square. Time: One minute per player.

Stationary: Practise throwing and receiving hooks. Time: Thirty seconds per player.

Station Two

Movement: The worker jumps laterally over a small cone five times then sprints forward to receive a straight pass. She throws it back to the thrower, returns to the cone and starts again. Time: One minute per player.

Stationary: Practise throwing and receiving shoulder passes. Time: One minute.

Station Three

Movement: The thrower stands on a transverse line and the worker starts on the baseline. The worker runs straight towards the thrower to receive a variety of passes. Time: One minute per player.

Stationary: Practise passing and receiving chest passes. Time: One minute.

Station Four

Movement: Set up four cones in a square about two metres apart. The worker sprints to the front left cone to receive a bounce pass, then back to the middle;

to the back left cone to receive a lob, then back to the middle; to the front right cone to receive a bounce pass, then back to the middle; and to the back right cone to receive a lob, then back to the middle. Time: One minute per player.

Stationary: Practise passing and receiving overhead passes. Time: One minute.

Station Five

Movement: The worker starts on one of the lines on the court with her back to the thrower, who is about three metres away. The thrower calls to the worker, throwing a reaction pass as she does so. The worker turns on the call and chases the reaction pass. Time: One minute per player.

Stationary: Practise reaction drops. The worker stands about metre away from the thrower with her hands touching her temples. The thrower stands with her arms out, holding the ball in both hands. The thrower drops the ball and the worker reacts to snatch it. The thrower should vary the height the ball drops from and the time between drops. Time: Thirty seconds per player.

Footwork

Passing and catching do not happen in isolation. In order to be in a position to catch the ball, a player must move. This involves some degree of footwork. Once she has the ball, a player cannot move until she passes the ball. This also involves some degree of footwork.

Speed of movement of the feet is a fundamental requirement for any player who wishes to improve her netball. All Commonwealth Bank Trophy teams will spend some time in the pre-season and during the season working on sprints and/or players' agility. As part of our home training program, the members of the Australian team do at least one speed session and one agility session per week. So you can see the importance that we place on our footwork. It is also important to ensure that the quality of our footwork doesn't deteriorate during the game. The more tired you become, the more you will have to concentrate on your feet during the game to ensure that they don't get sloppy.

The footwork required for netball can be broken up into three distinct phases: getting ready to move, moving and stopping. Let's take a look at each one separately.

Getting Ready to Move

As the ball moves down the court, a player must make certain preparations to either receive it or defend it. The optimum way to prepare for the short, sharp movement necessary to receive the ball is by moving the feet on the spot. This is commonly called 'pitter-patter' or 'fast feet' and involves moving the feet up and down in the one spot. The movement is not a big one — it can be no more than the player running on the spot by lifting her feet only a centimetre off the ground. The positioning of the feet is up to the individual. Some players like to pitter-patter with their feet shoulder-width apart. I prefer to pitter-patter in a running position, with one foot in front and one behind. That way, I am ready to move the moment my opposite number begins to run.

An alternative to the pitter-patter is bouncing on the balls of the feet. Former Australian goal defence and captain Michelle Den Dekker used to prepare to move by bouncing on her toes. Whilst this certainly worked for Michelle — she was an awesome defender — I decided against adopting this approach as it made me feel vulnerable because it gave my opponent a split second advantage if I was in the air when she moved.

Different things will work better for different people, so it is worth experimenting with the various ways of getting your feet ready to move as the ball comes towards you. There is no right or wrong way, just the way that best suits you.

A short exercise to get players thinking about their feet is to get them to stand on the baseline and pitter-patter. Once they are comfortable with this movement, the coach can then call 'left' or 'right', in which case the players move their left foot (if the call is 'left') out to the left, or their right foot (if the call is 'right') out to the right and back to the middle. The players then continue to pitter-patter and wait for the next call. Once they are proficient at this, the coach can call 'left front', 'right front', 'left back' or 'right back', in which case players step forward or back with the left or right foot as called.

The next step is for the players to practise their sprint-off from their pitter-patter by getting them to sprint out for five metres on a cue from the coach. The thing to look for when players sprint out is that they don't make their first step a backwards one. It sounds funny, but most people will actually make their first step a backwards one when they have to react to a call to sprint. The best explanation I can come up with is that the backwards step gives players some balance when they take their first step forward. If the backwards step can be eliminated it will add a good half-second to a player's speed. Half a second doesn't sound like much, but it translates to a full step faster over about ten metres.

A simple exercise to get a player to think about taking her first step forwards instead of back is to make her stand on the balls of her feet with her feet about shoulder-width apart and then get her to fall forwards. Once she feels that she is overbalancing, the player quickly moves a foot forward to stop herself falling. Once that first foot touches the ground, she then starts to sprint. This way, the player gets used to making her first step *forward* and she will eventually do it without having to lean forward.

This is another reason why I tend to pitter-patter in a running position with one foot forward and one back. I don't have to think about not putting my foot back before I go forward because I am already in a running position.

These footwork skills can be translated into a fun game by splitting the players into two groups and then lining up both groups facing each other down the length of the court. Each player pairs up with the player opposite her and they start by standing approximately three feet away from each other. Each line is given a name starting with the same letter — for example 'rats' and 'rabbits', or 'Swifts' and 'Sandpipers' (an increasingly popular choice!). When the coach calls 'rats', the rats turn and run to the sideline behind them, and the rabbits have to chase and try to tip the rats. If the coach calls 'rabbits', the rabbits turn and run to the sideline behind them with the rats giving chase. For the first couple of calls, the players should stand on the balls of their feet with their feet shoulder-width apart. This makes them concentrate on sprinting forwards without making their first step a backward one. This can then be progressed to the players pitter-pattering, and then to the coach calling 'left' or 'right', then 'left front', 'right front', 'left back' or 'right back'.

Moving

In a game situation, it will often be necessary for a player to make several moves before she receives the ball. She may make a straight lead, dodge, roll or a combination of each prior to getting the ball. The aim of each of these moves is, of course, to free the attacking player from the attentions of her defender. Some players are very efficient in their preliminary movements, and may only start to move just before they are to receive the ball. Players like Rebecca Sanders and Megan Anderson have speed to burn, so their preliminary movements can be limited to a few steps before they lose their defender. Other players start their preliminary movements well before the ball is in their third. I remember that after a game against Vicki Wilson, I would always come off feeling as if I had run a marathon because she always started her movements so early that I spent a vast majority of the game just running around after her.

A good habit to get into is mixing up the preliminary moves so that sometimes you begin your movement early and sometimes you move only a couple of steps. It is best to try to keep the defending player guessing which way you will go — and you don't want to show her your full bag of tricks early in the game.

Regardless of which preliminary move a player chooses, it is imperative that her final move is strong and towards the ball. The only time a player's final move should be away from the ball is if she has run forward and then put the brakes on to drop back into the space she has created by moving forwards.

All of these manoeuvres are ones that players should be able to carry out regardless of the position they play. These skills include the ability to perform a straight lead, dodge, double dodge, split, roll, clear, double play, hold and front cut.

Straight Lead

A straight lead is the best preliminary move for the ball because it is the simplest. It can be used when a player is not being closely defended, or when a player has a speed advantage over her defender. It is a move made in a straight line either directly or diagonally towards the ball. As a general rule, a straight lead should not be made directly sidewards. If there is no angle made towards the ball, the pass is susceptible to being intercepted by a defender between the attacker and the thrower.

Players can practise a straight lead with the following simple drill. You need three players — two will be throwers while one is the worker — and a ball. One thrower stands on one of the transverse lines and the other stands directly opposite her on the other transverse line. The worker starts with the ball and stands just in front of one of the throwers. She starts the drill by passing a shoulder pass to the thrower furthest away from her and then running straight at the thrower to receive a shoulder pass back from her. The worker then pivots and passes to the other thrower and sprints towards her to receive a pass. The worker repeats this two or three times before swapping with one of the throwers. The worker should ensure that she does not stop and wait for the ball to come to her, but rather that she sprints towards the ball until it is in her hands.

The next time the worker comes through, she starts a couple of metres to the right of one of the throwers and makes her straight lead diagonally left through the middle of the throwers, as shown in Figure 7.2.

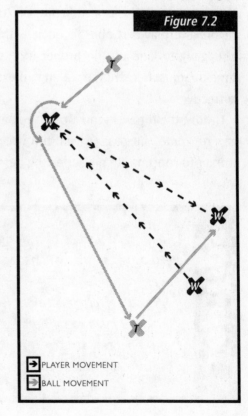

Figure 7.2

➡ PLAYER MOVEMENT
➡ BALL MOVEMENT

When she receives a shoulder pass from the thrower, she should try to land on her left foot and pivot around to the outside before passing to the other thrower and running back along the same diagonal. The final time the worker comes through, she does the same but this time she runs diagonally right and lands on her right foot.

There are a couple of things to keep in mind during this drill. Firstly, when the worker is running diagonally left or right, the angle should be at about 45° through the middle, rather than directly left or right. Two cones can be placed to make a diagonal line through the middle, to give the worker a spot to aim for when making her lead. If you do use the cones, get the worker to sprint in front of rather than behind the cones. This will get players used to running in front of rather than behind defenders.

Secondly, players should ensure that when they drive out to their left they land on their left foot, and when they drive out to their right they land on their right foot. This is a difficult skill to master, and it will take some practise before the player is able to do it without thinking about it. If the player is struggling to land on the proper foot, she should slow down so that she has time to adjust her stride by taking an extra step or two to ensure that she lands correctly.

Thirdly, the throwers must pass the ball out in front of the worker so that she can run onto the pass. A well-thrown pass will make it much easier for the worker to concentrate on perfecting her landing technique.

Top Tips

The first few steps of a straight lead must be short and explosive, so that you have an immediate advantage over your defender.

If you perform a straight lead, keep running strongly until you have caught the ball. If you slow down over your final few strides, it is likely that your defender will overrun you to take an intercept.

Dodge

Where a player dodges in order to lose her defender, she must ensure that her change of direction is sharp. Merely jogging, or moving around from one side to the other behind a defender will not deceive her. When the attacker moves to one side she must quickly shift her weight to the outside foot and back again in the opposite direction in the blink of an eye. In her initial movement, an attacking player needs to get the defender moving by making the defender think that the attacker is making a straight lead. The first movement should be made at close to top speed so that the defender commits to that direction. Further, a dodge by itself often will not be enough. Once a player has performed her dodge, she should then move onto the ball with her final steps.

Players can practise the necessary transfer of weight and foot speed for a dodge by setting up a series of cones in a zigzag, then running through the cones. Six or seven cones will be sufficient — they should be spaced between one and two metres apart. The player starts at one end of the cones and sprints to the first cone. Once she gets to the first cone, she changes direction on her outside foot and sprints to the next cone, and so on, changing direction each time on her outside foot. As a variation, the player may alternate between sprinting and sidestepping between the cones.

Some players may have trouble getting to each cone with their outside foot. If this is the case, they should take smaller strides so that each time they reach a cone they are able to push off with their outside foot. Players should also ensure that they are not taking one or two really big steps between the cones.

The next stage is to have a thrower stand a couple of metres in front of the last cone. After the player changes direction on the final cone, she drives out to receive a straight pass from the thrower.

Once the player has mastered the basic skill of transferring her weight onto her outside foot and back again, she is ready to practise the dodge itself. This can be done by using a variation on the drill for straight leads. Instead of sprinting diagonally all the way through the middle of the two throwers, the worker sprints diagonally to an imaginary straight line between the throwers. The worker changes direction at the line with her outside foot and sprints diagonally forwards in the other direction to receive a pass (see Figure 7.3). Once she receives the ball, she pivots, passes to the other thrower and goes again.

Once the player can perform a dodge on the run, she must practise dodging with no run-up. This is harder to do as the player must generate her momentum within a few steps. To practise this type of dodge, place two cones about one metre apart. A thrower stands a couple of metres in front of the cones, while the worker stands just behind, and midway between the cones (see Figure 7.4). The worker moves quickly to just behind the left cone, pushes off her left foot and sprints out in front of the right cone to receive the ball. She then does the same on the right side. Once the player is proficient at this, a defender can be placed in front of the cones so that the attacker gets used to moving fast enough to deceive the defender. At first the defender should only work at half pace, but build up to 100 per cent effort as the attacker gets better at dodging.

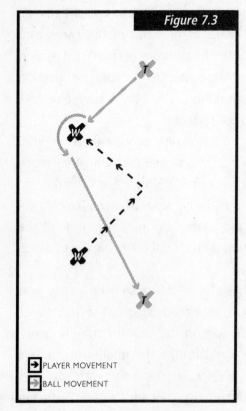

Figure 7.3

➡ PLAYER MOVEMENT

➡ BALL MOVEMENT

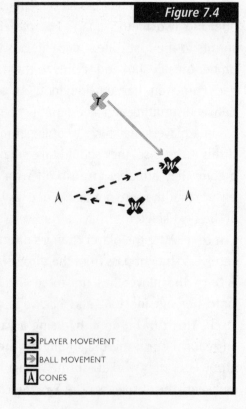

Figure 7.4

➡ PLAYER MOVEMENT

➡ BALL MOVEMENT

Λ CONES

Double Dodge

If the attacker does not shake the defender with just one change of direction, she may need to perform a second change of direction in order to free herself for the pass. The second change of direction is often effective, because once a defender has covered the first change of direction she will usually commit herself fully to the next move in order to get the intercept.

Practising a double dodge is reasonably easy once you have mastered the dodge. It is simply a matter of adding in another change of direction to the two drills outlined above. To practise the double dodge on the run, simply place a cone on the imaginary line between the two throwers of Figure 7.3. The worker sprints diagonally forward to the cone. When she reaches the cone, she changes direction on her outside foot, takes a couple of steps in the other direction, changes direction again on her outside foot (which will be the

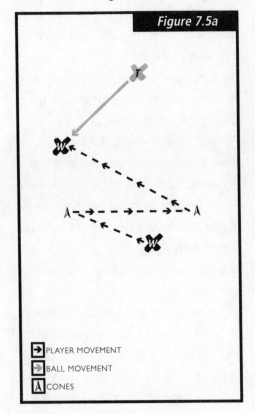

Figure 7.5a

PLAYER MOVEMENT

BALL MOVEMENT

CONES

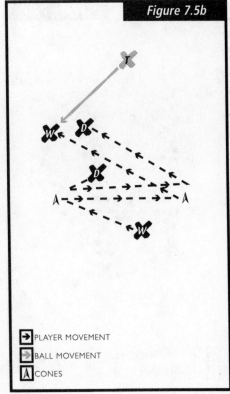

Figure 7.5b

PLAYER MOVEMENT

BALL MOVEMENT

CONES

opposite foot to the first change of direction) and then drives diagonally in front of the cone to receive a pass.

Next, place two cones about one metre apart. As she did when practising her single dodge, the worker starts by moving quickly to the left cone and pushes off her left foot to change direction, but instead of sprinting forward, the worker moves quickly to the right and pushes off her right foot. She then sprints out in front of the left cone to receive a pass as shown in Figure 7.5a. As the attacker becomes more proficient, a defender can be placed in front of the cones, working to cover the attacking movement as shown in 7.5b, initially at half pace and then moving to full pace.

Split

A split is a movement carried out by two players making a move for the same pass. It is particularly useful when players find themselves in close proximity to

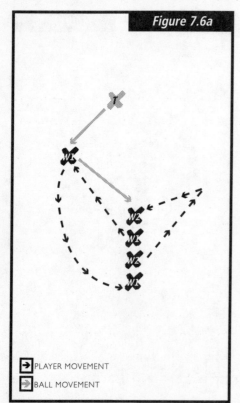

Figure 7.6a

PLAYER MOVEMENT
BALL MOVEMENT

each other and they both want to make an offer towards the ball. As the name suggests, a split involves the players starting together and running in opposite directions to give the thrower two options.

For a split to work, the front player must make her movement quick and decisive, while the back player must read the movement of the front player and adjust her own movement accordingly.

To practise a split, start with two or more players lined up one behind the other with the front player standing on the transverse line, and a thrower starting with the ball in the centre circle as shown in Figure 7.6a. The player at the front of the line leads

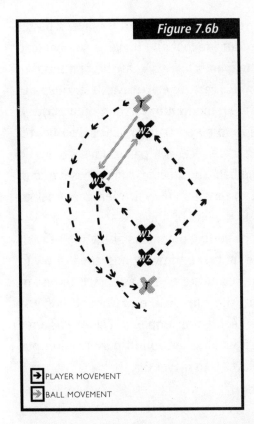

Figure 7.6b

PLAYER MOVEMENT

BALL MOVEMENT

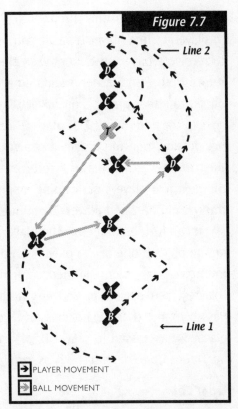

Figure 7.7

Line 2

Line 1

PLAYER MOVEMENT

BALL MOVEMENT

diagonally left or right, while the second player in the line leads diagonally forward in the opposite direction. The thrower then chooses one of the two leads to pass the ball to. The player who is not used changes direction on her outside foot as quickly as possible and sprints back to the top of the line to receive a pass from the player who did receive the ball. She then passes the ball back to the thrower and both workers go to the end of the line.

The next step is for the player who does not receive the ball to change direction on her outside foot and sprint to take the original thrower's position as shown in 7.6b. She then receives a pass from the player who first received the ball, and becomes the thrower for the next pair of players splitting.

The final part of this drill is splitting the team into two groups and lining each group up at diagonally opposite corners of the centre third (as shown in Figure 7.7). To start the drill, player T starts with the ball in the middle of the two lines and faces line 1. Players A and B split, and player T chooses one of those players to pass the ball to. After she throws, player T returns to line 2. If player T passes to player A, then player B pushes off her outside foot and makes a straight lead to receive a pass midway between the two lines. Player A, as the first receiver, returns to the end of her original line (in this case, line 1). Player B steadies and passes to either player C or player D, who are performing a split, then player B goes to the end of line 2. If player B passes to player D, then player C pushes off her outside foot and makes a straight lead to receive a pass midway between the two lines. When player C receives the ball, she steadies and chooses one of the next two players performing a split to pass to. Player D then goes back to the end of line 2 and player C continues to the end of line 1.

You can further challenge the players by adding defenders at the top of each line to pick up one of the players on the split. The thrower must then throw to the player who is undefended. After the second receiver has passed to one of the next two players performing a split, she runs to the player she has just passed to and defends her pass at three feet. For example, in Figure 7.7, after player B has passed to player D, player B would then run to player D and put her hands up to defend the pass from player D to player C.

Front Cut

A front cut is a particularly useful move for centre-court players as it allows them to use their speed to cut off the defender's line to the ball. However, it is a handy trick for all players to have up their sleeves. For example, if a player drives to the left side of the court, takes a pass, then turns and throws, she may try to make a front cut to the middle of the court as her next move. The front cut is quite simple. It involves the attacker drawing the defender in one direction and cutting around in front of her to drive to the ball. To do this, after releasing the ball, she would make a short lead to her right (and the defender's left) to drag the defender towards the sideline, which opens up the middle of the court. The attacker would then quickly push off her right foot to cut in front of the defender and run down the middle of the court.

It is easy to practise front cuts. Set up the 'split' drill as outlined in Figure 7.6a. Once the players are performing the drill comfortably, add in a defender whose job it is to pick up one of the players on the split. After the thrower has passed to the undefended player, the defended player cuts in front of the defender to take the ball in the middle of the two lines.

Double Play

As the name suggests, a double play is a movement where one player double-handles the ball with another player. It is often used in conjunction with a front cut. An example of a double play is where a wing attack receives the ball towards the side of the court, passes to the goal shooter, then front cuts to the top of the circle to receive the ball back from the goal shooter.

Rather than using a specific drill to practise double plays, it is a good idea to incorporate a double play into a normal ball-work drill. This is as simple as adding a double play into the free-flow drill outlined on page 81.

Roll

An attacking roll is an especially useful move for a goaler to master. To carry out a roll, the attacker moves a couple of steps in one direction then quickly performs a 180° outside turn to run in the opposite direction. When setting up for a roll, you should always allow plenty of space to move into. A roll is often used by the goaler to open up space behind her for a lob over the defender.

Once the attacker becomes proficient at performing a full roll, she can move onto a half roll. In this movement, the attacker gets halfway through the roll then moves back to the space she came from. This is a useful manoeuvre for when the defender moves back with the goaler on her initial roll, because once the defender is moving backwards it is difficult for her to transfer her body weight forwards to cover the second forward movement.

Clear

A clear is performed when a player shuffles backwards in a semicircle away from the thrower. It is important that she doesn't turn and run away from the ball, as this results in her losing sight of the ball. Rather, she should keep her eyes on the ball and move backwards. This gets her out of the space, but allows her to be in a position to make another lead towards the ball at any given time.

The length of the clear will depend on the space available to you and the situation you are in. For example, if you are a shooter and you have made a move towards the top of the circle that hasn't been used, you can either make a wide clear around the edge of the circle, or you can make a tight clear and move so that you end up close to the post. The thing to stress is that you should never take your eyes off the ball while performing your clear. You need to resist the urge to turn and run out of the space rather than sidestepping out of the way. You can almost guarantee that the moment you turn your head away from the ball, one of your team-mates will throw it to you!

A good drill to practise clearing is to get your team to line up down the court from goal post to goal post, as shown in Figure 7.8. The ball starts with player A. Player B sprints a couple of steps towards player A, then slows down and clears out of the space in a wide semicircle as shown. Player C sprints forwards to receive a straight pass from player A. Player C catches the ball, turns and passes to player B, who has timed her clear so that she covers the last couple of metres back towards the middle of the court at top pace. Player B turns and passes on to the next group, who repeat the clear and drive process.

Figure 7.8

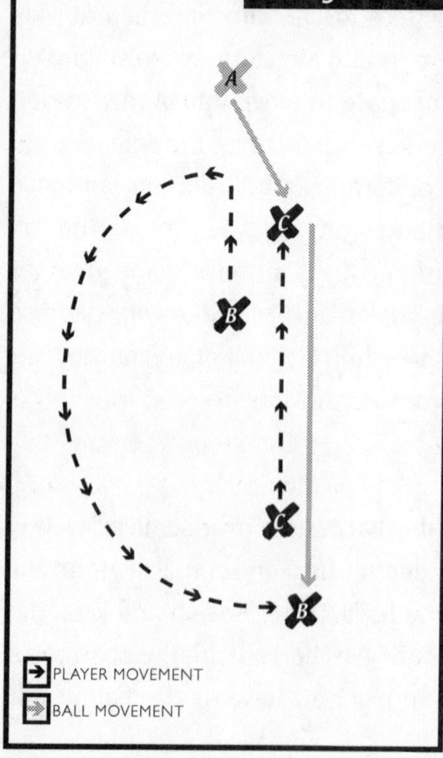

➡ PLAYER MOVEMENT
⟹ BALL MOVEMENT

Hold

A hold is used by an attacking player to hold space for the ball to be passed into. Any player on court can utilise a hold when they are attacking, although it is most often seen in the goal circle where a goaler will hold back or side space for a lob, or front space for a bounce pass. This is the only attacking manoeuvre which does not involve running, or some great deal of movement, to receive the ball. It does, however, require a certain degree of footwork. The player must continually move her feet and reposition her body to ensure that there is a clear space for her team-mates to throw the ball into.

The word 'hold' is a bit misleading, as the attacking player is not allowed to physically hold on to the defender to stop her from intercepting the ball. Rather, 'hold' refers to the attacker using her body to keep the defender's body away from the space she wants the ball passed into.

To perform a hold, take a reasonably wide stance — your feet should be slightly wider than shoulder-width apart — close to the defender. If you are holding for a lob, you should try to angle your body left or right so that the passer knows where to pass the ball.

When passing to a player who is holding space, you should always throw the ball to the space rather than to the player, as it is the space that the attacking player is holding which should be reasonably safe from the prying arms of the defenders. Throwing to the space also allows the holding player to move onto the ball. If the ball is thrown directly at the player, it forces the holding player into a one-on-one tussle for the ball, and allows the defender to have a go at intercepting the pass.

Players can practise holding with the following drill. Split into groups of three with one player as the attacker, one as the defender and one as the thrower. The thrower starts three or four metres away from the attacker. The attacker takes up a stance which allows her to hold space from the defender. To start with, the defender should stay reasonably static, so that the attacker can figure out how to hold space and the feeder can work out how to pass to that space. Next, the defender should start fairly still, but then have a go at the intercept when the ball is passed to the attacker. Finally, the defender should start moving around the attacker so that the attacker has to reposition her body and the feeder has to pick the right time to pass the ball.

Top Tips

1. A dodge does not always have to involve a couple of steps in either direction. You can move a single step in either direction, and move the upper half of your body from side to side, taking only a couple of steps towards the ball. You will need to have a good understanding with the player throwing to you as she will have to wait until the very last second before passing you the ball.

2. A double dodge is not necessarily the end of the line. If you have not freed yourself after the second dodge, try a third or fourth dodge. If, however, you haven't freed yourself by the third or fourth dodge, then you may need to utilise another preliminary movement, or perform a clear so that one of your team-mates can make use of the space you are in.

3. The key to an effective split is a fast initial movement by both players, and a sharp change of direction by the second player.

4. All of the preliminary movements can be used in conjunction with each other. Try stringing a few together to free space for yourself or for another player. But don't confuse the matter by putting on too many movements to get the ball. As I said earlier, a straight lead is the best because it is the simplest.

5. Mix up the type and number of preliminary moves you do, so that you keep the defender guessing. If you always dodge left and lead right, the defender won't have much trouble working this out and covering the movement. If, on the other hand, you mix up the movements, you will keep some degree of doubt in the defender's mind.

Stopping

Once you have received the ball, you need to be able to stop so that you don't infringe the footwork rule. When you have the ball in your hands, you are permitted to take only one and a half steps before you have to throw it. This means that you may lift your grounded foot after catching the ball, but may not put it down before releasing it. You are free to move the foot that is not your grounded foot while you have the ball. This allows you to pivot on the grounded foot to assess your options before passing.

One important thing to remember about stopping is that it is important for you to cushion your landing by bending your knees as your feet come into contact with the ground. This will help you to avoid wear-and-tear injuries to your knees and ankles.

A simple drill for practising stopping is the second drill outlined on page 46. While it is important in that drill for the player to run hard at the thrower until she has the ball in her hands, it is also imperative that the player learns to stop once she has caught the ball. This drill can also be extended to include the skill of pivoting. To do this, a second thrower is added opposite the first. The worker throws to the first passer and runs directly at her to receive the ball. Once she receives the ball, she must stop, pivot on her grounded foot, and pass to the second thrower. The worker then runs straight at the second thrower, receives, stops, pivots and throws back to the first. The worker should alternate stopping and pivoting with each foot as the grounded one.

Once the player is comfortable with this drill, it can be varied to challenge the player further. The throwers stay as they were above, but now the worker drives diagonally forward to the left to receive the ball, concentrating on landing on her left foot. She then pivots to the outside on her grounded foot and passes to the second thrower, runs to her to receive, stops, pivots and goes again. The worker repeats this process, driving out to her right.

The next step is for the worker to start in the middle of the two throwers, drive diagonally left, receive the ball, pivot and pass to the other thrower. Once she releases the ball, the worker drives back to the middle, changes direction

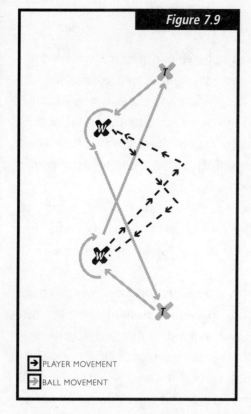

Figure 7.9

PLAYER MOVEMENT

BALL MOVEMENT

quickly, and drives out to the right to receive the ball, pivot and pass (see Figure 7.9).

There are several important things to remember during this drill. The first is that the worker must concentrate on landing on her left foot when she is driving to her left, and on her right foot when driving out to her right. Once she lands on the correct foot, the worker needs to concentrate on pivoting to the outside. For example, when the worker runs to her left and lands on her left foot, she pivots anticlockwise. When the worker drives right and lands on her right foot, she pivots clockwise.

The next step is to get the players used to catching and passing on the run. It is important that players can mix up the speed at which they catch and pass the ball. Sometimes it is necessary for a player to stop, take in her options and then pass. This usually happens when things start to get a little out of control as the ball comes down the court. If a player can steady herself before she passes, this will have the effect of steadying her team-mates and help to get the game back in control. At other times, it is necessary for a player to be able to catch and pass in one motion. This skill is important when her team has a 'fast break' down the court and wants to get the ball from one end to the other in a hurry.

In a Commonwealth Bank Trophy or international match, you can see that the players are able to move the ball quickly down the court because they can catch and pass without stopping. When using this move, it is important that the player gets rid of the ball before she regrounds her landed foot. It is also important that she makes it clear to the umpires which foot is her grounded foot. This has been something the Australian Netball Team has had to do, as umpires from other countries, where the style of play is different, often aren't used to the speed at which the ball travels or the speed of our foot movement.

One thing that you can do to practise catching and passing in one motion is to pair up and, beginning on the baseline, run the full length of the court passing the ball between you and your partner without stopping. Ensure that you keep control of both the ball and your feet, and run so that your passes are different lengths and speeds. This way, you get used to picking your team-mates' speed as well as regulating your own.

Chapter 8

Teamwork

In 1995, Debbie Hammond, captain of the South African team, paid the Australian team an enormous compliment moments after we defeated her team by twenty goals in the World Championship final. When asked why the Aussie team had been so dominant in that game, her response was that we play 'as one'. What she meant was that we were not just seven players making up a netball team, but rather a single unit made up of seven parts doing our own jobs. I took this comment as a great compliment to our team because to behave 'as one' is the ultimate expression of what a team is. It is also something that is extremely difficult to achieve.

For a team to behave 'as one' they need to have a thorough understanding of each other's style of play. Often when a play breaks down on court, it is due to the fact that there is a misunderstanding between the thrower of the pass and her intended recipient. Understanding is developed in a number of ways. Firstly, through sheer hard work. Players will only get used to each other after they have thrown the ball to each other hundreds of times in various situations. Secondly, players must have a good awareness of their own space and the space of their team-mates. Thirdly, players need to be given a team objective to work towards and they must understand what their role in this is.

Sheer Hard Work

It sounds a bit dramatic, but in actual fact, hard work is absolutely necessary. There is very little point in a team developing complicated tactics or dazzling moves if they have not done the required groundwork so that each player in the team is fully aware of the capabilities of her team-mates. Each player in the team needs to know who she can throw the ball hard to, and who needs a gentler touch on the pass; she must understand that some players have a blistering turn of speed, yet others have a slower, steadier pace. This is not to say that the team must cater to the weaknesses of each player, but rather that the team should discover and capitalise on each player's strengths. The elimination of weaknesses is something that can be worked on throughout the season.

The first step of 'sheer hard work' is to ensure that each player in the team has a firm grasp of the basics. Each player must be able to catch, pass, and control her feet. If a player is having difficulties in this area, it may be that she needs to be given a little individual attention from the coach, either before, after, or separate from team training sessions. If this is the case, the extra training should be done in a sensitive way, to ensure that the player does not feel singled out or embarrassed. Perhaps if she has a friend in the team they could both take part in any extra training so that it is fun for them both. It is so important that netball is fun for each of the players in a team. I can guarantee that there is no way I would do all of the work required to be in the Australian team if I didn't have fun when I got there!

The second step is to get the team doing their ball-work drills well. There are plenty of drills in which players must move, catch and pass. One of my favourite ones is beautiful in its simplicity. Place three cones five metres apart in an 'L' shape. Split the players into two even groups. The first group forms a

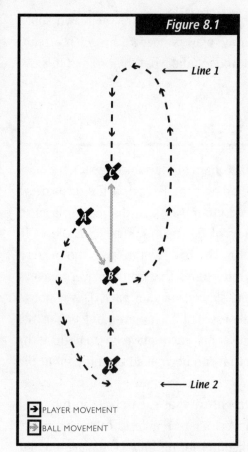

Figure 8.1

← Line 1

← Line 2

→ PLAYER MOVEMENT

→ BALL MOVEMENT

line at one end of the 'L' and the second group forms a line at the other end of the 'L'. The ball starts with the player at the front of one line. The player at the front of the other line sprints to the cone in the middle of the 'L' and receives a straight, hard pass from the player with the ball. She catches the ball, pivots and passes it back to the next person in her line. She then runs back to the end of her line. The first player in the opposite line then runs to the middle cone, receives a pass from the second line, turns and passes to the next person in her line, and runs back to the end of her line. This drill can be done over a smaller area to start with, so that the passes are accurate, and then a bigger area as the players become more proficient. There are plenty of variations, such as getting the players to dodge before they sprint, or getting them to dodge just before they receive a pass from the player in the middle.

In a similar drill, one group lines up one behind the other starting at the transverse line (line 1), facing the centre circle, and the other group lines up directly opposite the first group (line 2) starting on the other transverse line as shown in Figure 8.1.

Player A starts with the ball in the middle of the two lines. Player B sprints towards player A and receives a straight pass from her. Once player A has thrown, she runs through to the end of line 2. Player B steadies herself and passes to player C, who is running straight towards her. Once player B has passed the ball, she runs to the end of line 1. Player C passes to the next player in line 2 and so on.

This drill is a useful one because it can have plenty of variations. For example, you can:

▶ bring the lines closer together and use lobs or bounce passes;

▶ get the players to make their lead diagonally left or diagonally right;

▶ alternate the left and right leads — for example, if player A leads left, then player B leads right;

▶ get players to dodge before they make their lead; or

▶ put one or two players in the middle to defend those players making the leads.

The final point is pretty important — I believe that all drills should be done for a purpose, not just to fill in the time at training. This means that where possible, drills should replicate a game situation. Adding one or two defenders into a drill is a really good way of doing this because it forces players out of their comfort zone (where they can perform drills without thinking about them) and into a situation where they have to think and respond quickly. However, defenders should be added to a drill only after the team is able to perform the initial exercise easily, as it is necessary to give players a feel for what is required of them before introducing obstacles.

An important point to remember when doing these drills, and, in fact, every team drill, is that players must concentrate on their timing. A player should not leave her line and make a move until the player passing to her has caught the ball, steadied herself, and is ready to pass. Timing is a vital part of a team's performance on court, and it's something that players should work on. If a player leads to the ball too early in a game situation, it will throw out the whole attacking play, as it forces everyone to readjust their moves. Also, if a player leads too early and then has to stand and wait for the ball to come to her, there is a good chance that it will be intercepted. Speaking from a defender's point of view, there is nothing that advertises where an intercept can be taken more than a player standing still and waiting for the ball to get to her. If you take a look at any of the Commonwealth Bank Trophy matches, you will see that very few players stand and wait for the ball. Most passes are thrown to, and caught by, players on the move.

Once players begin to concentrate on other things such as timing, or throwing to a player who is on the move or who is defended, it is important that their basic skills don't begin to suffer. Younger players in particular need to be reminded of their footwork or of the need to throw a strong shoulder pass when they are in an on-court situation that requires them to think about a number of things at once. One way to reinforce the need to concentrate on basic skills is to remind the players that they each have a responsibility to catch the ball safely, steady their feet and then give their team-mates a good strong pass.

So, 'sheer hard work' is about doing the little things well and getting the players familiar with their team-mates. There are any number of drills that you can do that get players used to throwing the ball to their team-mates and working off each other's movement. Once players have mastered some simple dills, you should then move on to drills that have a component of uncertainty, where players have to react to someone or something. These types of drills are excellent to get teams used to each other's timing.

There are many available in netball coaching manuals. Don't be afraid to tweak these drills to suit your team, and don't be afraid to introduce defensive pressure into a drill. Finally, if you do make up your own drills, try to keep them simple.

Top Tips

1. *If you or a team-mate fumble a ball in a drill, run to pick it up and keep the drill going — this is what you will have to do if it happens in a game.*
2. *Try to set your team targets for the drills. For example, try to do a drill for thirty seconds without a fumble and then, going up by five or ten second increments, increase this to a minute.*
3. *Never finish a drill on a drop or a fumble. Team morale will be much stronger if each drill finishes on a positive note.*

Space Awareness

Space awareness is all about knowing what space is available to you and what space your team-mates want to use. It is more than knowing *where* you can go on the netball court. Rather, space awareness is about players knowing where you *should* go. Younger players in particular have a tendency to run straight to where the ball is. This results in a situation where you could throw a large handkerchief near the ball and manage to cover most of the players on the court!

When I started playing netball, I was a real ball hog — I was the player most likely to run into the middle of the mess rather than try and do something about it. That is until my mum took me to watch the local A-Grade competition and pointed out to me that the big girls used the whole court when they were trying to get the ball from one end to the other. This opened up a whole new world for me, as I realised that if you wanted the ball you were better off running to a space, rather than at the ball.

It is really difficult to 'coach' players to realise what is going on around them. There is one drill I like doing that gets players thinking about making use of the whole space available to them — but be warned, it is possible that players can run into each other and hurt themselves, so warn them before you start that they need to keep an eye out for their team-mates.

Start by splitting the players into four even groups. Move each group to separate corners of the centre third, and line the players up behind one another from just outside the corner and facing the centre circle. When you call 'go' or blow your whistle, the first player in each line sprints to the corner diagonally opposite her and joins the end of that line. Keep going until each player has had a couple of sprints through the middle. Once the players can do this without running into each other, take a ball and throw it into the middle of the third while the players are running. The players must react to the pass and chase down the ball. Once a player gets the ball, she must steady her feet and pass it back to you before continuing to her opposite corner. The remaining players continue running through to their opposite corner.

Do this a couple of times until the players get used to running through the centre third while keeping their eye on both the ball and each other. Then progress the drill so that the player who first picks up the ball steadies her feet and then passes to one of the three other players who are in the middle third. Do this a couple of times, then extend it so that there are two passes (in which case there will be one player who doesn't receive the ball), and then finally three passes, so that each of the four players in the centre third receives the ball.

So where does the space awareness come in? It comes into play in two ways. The first is when the players are running through the centre third. They must be aware not only of where they want to go but also where the other players are in relation to them, and adjust their speed accordingly. Secondly, when the players have to pass to each other, they must be encouraged to use the whole third. To get them to do this, prevent the player with the ball from passing it to one who is standing still. Also, a player who wants the ball must keep making leads until she receives a pass. For example, if a player wants the ball, she must make a lead the moment the first player picks up the ball. If she is not used for the first pass, she must make another lead in another direction in an attempt to get the second pass. If she is not used for the second pass, she has to make a third lead in a different direction again for the last pass. This should see the last player use most of the space in the third.

Once the players have mastered the skill of using all the space available to them when they are confined to one third, it is then time to get them thinking about using it all the way down the court. This can be done by way of 'free flow', where the players take the ball from one end of the court to the other and back again with very little structure, which means that there are no set positions or stations for the players to work from or run to, but rather they decide where to go based on where their team-mates are. To do this, split the players up into three reasonably even groups. There needs to be one group of goalers, one of centre-court players and one of defenders. These groups are fairly fluid, so it doesn't matter if a goaler or defender is pushed into the centre-court group or vice versa. Each group starts in a different third, with the centre-court group taking the middle third and the goalers and defenders a goal third each.

The ball starts with one of the defenders who signals the start of the drill by tossing the ball in the air and catching it. The other defenders must then make a lead in preparation for a pass. If, for example, there are two other defenders in the third, the thrower will have two leads in different directions to choose from. The thrower chooses one of these leads to pass to. The recipient catches the ball, steadies and passes to the third defender, who must change the direction of her lead to receive the ball. Once each of the players in the defensive third has received the ball, the last player looks to the centre third to off-load the ball. As she does this, she must receive a lead from each of the centre-court players. Each player in the centre third must handle the ball, making a new lead every time the ball is thrown. Once they have done that, the last player with the ball looks to the shooting third. Each goaler handles the ball, with the last goaler receiving a pass in the circle and taking a shot. Regardless of whether she is successful, she then rebounds the ball, which starts the drill again, and the ball travels back up the court in the same manner. Once each defender has handled the ball on its return up the court, the drill is finished, although it can be extended by having the last defender take a shot and starting again from the rebound.

This is an important drill for players to master, as it gets them comfortable with using the whole court, and helps them to read the moves being made by their team-mates. To this end, players should be aware that for every opportunity to pass the ball there should be a short, medium and long offer. Making these multiple offers is something that players should always do during a game and this drill is an excellent way to get them thinking about it. At the very least, there should be two, and preferably three, offers to each pass on court. It doesn't create much doubt in the minds of the defending players if only one offer is made for the ball. While it is difficult during a match to be able to assess in less than three seconds where the short, medium and long leads should be, it is something that can be practised with this drill. It is also something that can be done fairly simply by getting the players to work from a simple formula — the player closest to the ball makes the first move. If this is a short lead, then the players behind her must read that and adjust their leads accordingly.

By short, medium and long leads I mean, respectively, a move towards the thrower within a couple of metres of the ball, a move about five metres from the ball, and a move about ten metres from the ball. Obviously, these distances will vary depending upon where the player with the ball is standing. For example, if a defender has taken an intercept and is struggling to regain her balance, there may be two short and one medium offer. As a rule, though, each of the options should be different distances — preferably in different directions.

'Free flow' also gets players thinking about reoffering for the ball. When a player makes a move and is not used, she should not just stop where she is and wait for the game to move on. She needs to initiate another move. She can make a straight drive in another direction or, if she is reasonably close to the ball and taking up space that could be better utilised by someone else, she will need to clear out so that one of her team-mates can drive into that prime position.

Therefore, it is necessary that players not only think about using all of the space available to them on the netball court, but also that they begin to think about opening up space for their team-mates to utilise.

Once your players are able to do basic 'free flow' without too much trouble, you can start to vary it by:

▶ Getting the players to sprint forward as a reoffer after they pass the ball. It doesn't matter if the player has to go into the next third to do this.

▶ Making every second pass a bounce pass or a lob, which the recipient has to run onto (i.e. she cannot just stand and wait for the ball to come to her).

▶ Making the first play in each third a double play. This can be done by having the first recipient in each third double play with the person they received the ball from in the previous third, or having the first recipient double playing with the second recipient in her third.

▶ Making the first pass in each third back to the previous third — the first player to receive the ball in each third passes it back to any player in the previous third and then clears out of the way for the other players in her third to drive towards the ball.

▶ Occasionally calling 'down' or 'drop', in which case the player with the ball drops it at her feet and clears away from the ball. One of the other players in her third must react and sprint to the ball and pick it up. This will require a degree of communication between the players so that only one person runs at the ball. Generally a call of 'mine' or 'got it' should be sufficient to alert team-mates that a player intends to get the ball. This call should come from the player closest to the ball.

▶ Making the first pass into each third a reaction pass, so that the players in the next third have to move, communicate and read off each other to retrieve the ball and create the next play.

▶ Adding a defender to float around in each third.

The next step along from 'free flow' is developing court systems. This is essentially a more structured version of 'free flow'. It is one of the things that the Australian Netball Team and the Sydney Swifts do as part of our training. Practising court systems is a good way to conclude a training session as it is quite specific and gets the players thinking about timing and reading their team-mates. Generally, court systems are begun from a throw-in situation with the goal keeper starting with ball, although they can be moved down the court to start from the goal third or with a sideline throw-in in the centre court. While this type of drill is initiated by a throw-in, it is not necessarily throw-in practice. Rather, it is practising bringing the ball down court from a defensive turnover.

So while court systems don't necessarily have to start from a throw-in, it is as good a place as any to begin. For something different, the coach or another player can throw a reaction ball onto the court, which the players have to chase down, and the system can start from there.

To start a full-court system, you will need to have seven players on court in their positions, standing roughly where they would start on a centre pass, although this would depend on where the goal keeper takes the throw-in from. (If the goal keeper takes a throw-in from the sideline, the goal defence, wing defence and centre will need to adjust their starting positions by moving down the court to provide the goal keeper with options in front, rather than behind her.) An example of starting positions for a throw-in from the defence

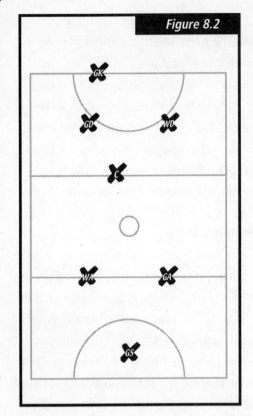

Figure 8.2

baseline is shown in Figure 8.2. Remember, this is just a guide and modifications may need to be made to fit your team objectives, and the capabilities and playing style of each player.

The reason why the players should start in these positions is that it gives each one her own space to work in. If the wing attack or goal attack starts too high, she will crowd the defenders' attacking space. In order to make sure that the goal attack and wing attack are free to work the ball into the goal circle, the defenders should be used to bring the ball down the court as much as possible. If the goal attack is standing up on the transverse line of the opposition's goal third, she will not only impede the defenders' attacking roles but she will also unbalance the rest of the team's attacking play, as her positioning will force the wing attack and the goal shooter to come up the court to fill the space. This means that once the ball is in the goal third, there are fewer attacking options.

To start off the court system, the goal keeper throws the ball in from anywhere along the baseline. As she steps up to the line, the rest of the team take their positions and begin to make offers. As a general rule, the goal keeper will look to the wing defence or goal defence as her first option. If she is standing on the right-hand side of the post (looking down the court), then the goal defence, starting from her position as shown in Figure 8.2, will be her first option. The goal defence should decide in which direction to make an offer to the goal keeper based on where the opposition's goal attack is. If the goal attack is in front of her, she can either hold for a lob into the corner of the third, or she can dodge and make a lead to the goal keeper. If the goal attack is behind the goal defence, the goal defence can hold her ground to receive a pass that drops just in front of her.

If the goal shooter has dropped back to help the goal attack defend the goal defence, then the goal defence should clear out of that space. This will not only open up the space for another player to move into, but it may also get rid of her two defenders (the goal attack and goal shooter) as they should follow her out of the space. If this happens, or if the goal defence can't take the pass for another reason, the next option is the wing defence. When a throw-in is on the goal defence's side of the court, the wing defence should hold as closely to the top of the circle as possible. This makes her a reasonably safe option.

A golden rule of baseline throw-ins is that the goal defence should avoid leading into, and the goal keeper should avoid throwing into, the goal circle. This is because if the ball is intercepted by the goal attack or the goal shooter, they will inevitably take a shot. If the ball is intercepted outside the circle, the defenders at least get a chance to put up some resistance before the shot is taken.

If the throw-in is taken on the left-hand side of the post (looking down the court), the first option is the wing defence. At times like this, the circle is the wing defence's best friend. The wing defence should set up for throw-ins on her side of the court on the edge of the circle with her feet slightly wider than shoulder-width apart. This position makes her a fairly easy target for the goal keeper to pass to. The goal keeper should aim to pass slightly to the side that doesn't have the wing attack defending. If the goal shooter drops back to defend, the wing defence should clear out of that space to let another player utilise it. If the throw-in is on, or close to, the sideline then it is impractical for the wing defence to set up on the circle — she will need to hold space behind or in front of her for the goal keeper to throw the ball into.

Once the goal defence or wing defence has the ball, then she can look to the centre driving down court or (if she is the goal defence), the wing defence, or (if she is the wing defence), the goal defence driving down court, or the wing attack or goal attack making a lead towards her. If the goal defence or wing defence has the ball reasonably close to the circle, she may look to double play back to the goal keeper. To this end, the goal keeper should always ensure that she makes a lead to make herself available after she has thrown the ball in.

I prefer to make my lead as close to the transverse line as I can so that I have plenty of options. If both the wing defence and goal defence are unavailable, the next option is the centre. As the throw-in is taken, the centre must be aware that she may be needed. It should only take a glance in her direction from the goal keeper to get her moving. The best lead she can make is straight down the middle of the court. If she does this, when she has to pass the ball on, there should be plenty of options for her to choose from, two of which should be the goal defence and wing defence. One of my favourite options when I receive the ball close to the transverse line is to look to the wing attack. The wing attack should be standing reasonably close to the opposite transverse line as I take the ball. From there, she makes a short lead forward to receive the ball. One thing that former Australian Netball Team vice-captain Sue Kenny used to do when she was playing wing attack was to make her first step across and in front of the wing defence, which essentially stopped her defender from having a go at the intercept. It also meant that she only needed to take a couple of steps forward onto the ball instead of making a really long lead. The beauty of this pass is that it clears the ball out of the defence third and quickly sets up the next attacking movement.

Once the ball is out of the defensive third it should move reasonably quickly through the centre third. To get the wing attack and goal attack used to waiting for the defenders to bring the ball to them, they should not make a lead until the ball is near the centre circle. If the defenders are in trouble or looking for a long outlet pass, they can make a lead earlier, although they should not get into the habit of doing this and ending up past the centre circle. Similarly, the goal shooter should not lead out of the circle until the ball is close to the transverse line and is in her third. If the goal defence or wing defence has the ability to throw a long shoulder pass, you can also think about having the goal shooter lead out of the circle, and quickly putting on the brakes and then sprinting back into the circle as the defender catches the ball near the transverse line. If the goal keeper commits to the intercept on the outward lead, the pass is reasonably simple (if long).

ABOVE: The Hawkesbury Under-Twelves were my second representative team. I'm in the back row, third from the right, with a haircut that makes me cringe! Our coach Helen Lane, on the right, was an enormous influence on me during those early years.

ABOVE: Maria Lynch, coach for the Under-Seventeen NSW Team, reminding me to throw the ball to the players wearing light blue. (I think I went overboard with the hair ribbons!)

ABOVE: One of the reasons the NSW Open Team was successful for so long was because we all got along very well. We are at a function in New Zealand after our coach told us we were to 'keep ourselves nice'.

ABOVE: The sign says it all. At Sydney Town Hall in 1999 after our ticker-tape parade though the city.

ABOVE: How were we going to pull this one off? The Aussie team talking tactics during a time-out in the final of the 1999 World Netball Championships.

RIGHT: No, it's not a new dance! New Zealand goal shooter Donna Loffhagen and I had a pretty physical contest in the 1999 World Netball Championships final. I guess I won this particular clash.

RIGHT: One of my good friends, Cath Cox, catching the ball strongly during a warm-up.

Allsport: Ruth Gray

Allsport: Ruth Gray

LEFT: Catriona Wagg and Karen Miller form a formidable defence for the Sydney Swifts against Karen Clarke from the Brisbane Firebirds.

ABOVE: A rare rebound against Vicki Wilson. We are great friends off the court and we were great opponents on it!

ABOVE: Jenny Borlase shows all of the concentration required to be a top-class goaler. Here she is playing for Australia in a match against England.

LEFT: I love taking these sorts of intercepts — the ball is in the air and I get to have a fly!

Allsport: Nick Wilson

Allsport: Nick Wilson

RIGHT: I don't mind scrapping for the ball, either! England's Lyn Carpenter and I fight for possession.

RIGHT: I'm trying to put South Africa's Irene van Dyk off her shot during the 1995 World Netball Championships final. Our captain and goal defence Michelle Den Dekker looks on.

LEFT: It is a great feeling to tip a goaler's shot. Don't feel sorry for Melbourne Phoenixes' Eloise Southby though — despite my best efforts, she has shot plenty of goals against me in the Commonwealth Bank Trophy competition!

Once the ball reaches the goal third, the attack line must work it into a shot. Again, players should not be waiting for the ball to get to them. Each lead should be strong and preferably towards the ball. To practise doing this, the attackers can be set different tasks in this drill. For example, they may have to pass the ball in and around the circle ten times before they can shoot, or they may have to shoot from where they first receive the ball in the circle.

The next step is to prevent players from converging onto the player with the ball during the game. Doing 'free flow' and court system drills should get players used to thinking about their space and the space of their team-mates. If players are still running into a big bunch, it may be useful to take some video footage of the game so that they can see where they are running to in a game can then be shown what space they should be utilising instead.

Top Tips

1. *If you want the ball, run to a space rather than to the ball.*
2. *Video a Commonwealth Bank Trophy or international test match and watch closely what the person playing your position is doing. This will give you an idea of the space you should use in your position.*

Team Objective

Each time the team walks onto the court for a match, the players should have a team objective in mind. This objective should be specific to the game they are about to play and clearly spell out the roles of each player. The objective may include something as simple as aiming to score a certain number of goals and restricting the opposition to a certain number of goals. However, it may also include a strategy to stop a particular opposition player from being dominant, or a plan to exploit any perceived weaknesses in the opposition. How familiar you are with your opponents will determine the nature of the team's objective.

The objective should not be aimed at vastly altering the team's style of play from week to week, but rather it should seek to direct the team's style to a specific game plan. This can be incorporated into an overall season strategy which should be clearly spelt out at the start of the year.

Once the team has its objective in mind, each individual player needs to be directed as to how they are to help the team meet its objective. To this end, players should go onto the court with a couple of goals to work towards during the game. I generally take a couple of moments out a few hours prior to most matches to think about what I want to achieve during the game, and how that fits into what the team is trying to achieve. Often my goals are fairly simple, and I always try to make them realistic, so that I can walk off the court satisfied that I have achieved what I set out to do or knowing what I have to do to improve my performance in the next match. These individual goals can range from moving my feet to have a go at a high ball, to mixing up my defence of the shot, through to getting one intercept and two rebounds per quarter. They may also be as simple as having a good warm-up, or remaining focused if I am starting the game on the bench.

The coach should be aware of each player's goals, so that she can provide feedback during and after the game as to whether the goals have been achieved and if they have, what the next task is for the player. This way, each player will improve their performance week by week, which will have a flow-on effect on the team's performance.

It is worth noting here that a team very rarely goes through a season undefeated. In fact, in my first few years of netball, my teams very rarely won. It is often difficult when a season isn't going so well to keep up team morale and continue to train hard. If this is the case, then having a team objective may help everyone keep their spirits up, because it may be that, even if they lose, the team will end up achieving something — which almost makes up for the loss. This is when it is most important to have fun. It doesn't matter what the score is if you are having a good time!

I also believe that losing teaches you a lot more than winning. I remember a few years ago, after we had lost (to New Zealand) our first test match in several years, Joyce Brown sent us all a quote which I have kept on my wall at home. I don't know who wrote it, but it says:

We learn far more from failure than from success. We often find out what will do by finding out what will not do. And she who never made a mistake, never made a discovery.

This is such an important — but difficult — thing to realise. Every time you lose, or don't perform well, either individually or as a team, you learn something. That's why I cringe when someone says to me that they are going to change teams or clubs because their team is not very good and they don't win. I spent the majority of my early netball career in teams that didn't win, and I benefited enormously from it. Not only does it teach you to lose graciously, but it also makes you more determined to do well next time you play — and it makes victory so much sweeter when you do get to taste it!

Top Tips

1. **At the end of a game, write down what did and didn't work against your opponents. This will allow you to better plan for your next encounter.**
2. **Start the year with a team objective. Get the team together and brainstorm so that you come up with a mission statement for the year. This will help you remain focused throughout the year.**

Chapter 9

Shooting

There is no way I would be a goaler! Sure, they get all of the glory — whenever netball highlights get shown on television it is always goalers shooting goals and defenders standing around looking useless — but they are also the first people to get the blame when the team loses. It is much easier to blame a goaler for missing a shot than it is to blame a defender for missing an intercept or a centre-court player for missing a feed. Missed shots are easily measurable — missed feeds and intercepts aren't!

To add insult to injury, they always have to go to training earlier than everyone else to practise their shots. When I was at the Australian Institute of Sport in Canberra, I almost felt sorry for the goalers as they trotted off to training half an hour earlier than everyone else. Now when we are away with the Australian team and the goalers have to get up early to go and shoot on our morning off, I just enjoy the warmth of my bed for that extra time.

Don't get me wrong, I am always trying to get Jill McIntosh and Julie Fitzgerald — respectively, the Australian and Sydney Swifts coaches — to give me a turn at goal shooter. Unfortunately for my shooting aspirations, both coaches have the good sense to roll their eyes and ignore me when I am carrying on in such a manner.

One of the reasons they can both afford to take no notice of my pleas to be given a turn as goal shooter is the enormous depth of talent Australia has in this area. This was no more evident than when the Australian team took on New Zealand in June 2000 in what was a replay of the 1999 World Championships final. Of the four goalers who took the court for Australia in the 1999 final, the only one remaining in the Australian team in 2000 was Sharelle McMahon. Vicki Wilson and Jenny Borlase had both retired, and goal attack Jacqui Delaney had suffered a season-ending knee injury at the beginning of the year. Enter Cath Cox, Eloise Southby and Megan Anderson, with the grand total of eight test caps between them. As the most experienced goaler in the team, twenty-two-year-old Sharelle McMahon, with twenty-five caps to her name, was hardly a seasoned veteran.

None of this mattered. From the opening whistle Sharelle ruled the roost in our goal circle, ably assisted first by Eloise and then by Cath. Cath Cox, in particular, must have really annoyed the Kiwi defenders. It was her first game against New Zealand and she was outstanding. To make matters worse, it was only a twist of fate that had her shooting goals for Australia — you see, she was born in New Zealand, and even though she moved over here with her parents when she was young, she didn't get an Australian passport until she was eighteen and was selected to play in the NSW Open Team for the first time. We gave her such a hard time when she pulled out a New Zealand passport at Sydney airport to go to New Zealand for some training matches that she became an Australian citizen the very next opportunity she got.

So, if anyone had any doubts as to how Australia would cope with filling the gaping hole left by Wilson and Borlase, they were quickly dispelled by the arrival of the new guard. These players are following in the footsteps of great goalers like Anne Sargeant, Sue Hawkins and Margy Caldow — who caused plenty of problems for opposition defenders over many years.

The most important thing for a goaler is accuracy. While some players may have a natural ability to shoot well, that will only take them part of the way. It is absolutely vital that goalers practise shooting. Sure, it involves extra work, but it is worth it, given that everyone's focus is on the goalers and whether they are successful or not.

To give you an idea of what is required, most goalers will put up at least 300 shots a week, although the number varies greatly from player to player. Vicki Wilson used to shoot 200 goals a day six days a week to keep her eye in — on a good day it took her twenty minutes, and on a bad day up to an hour. Jenny Borlase used to put up 100–150 goals three times a week before training. Of the current Australian squad goalers, Eloise Southby is the most prolific, with 250 goals a day, five days a week, followed by Megan Anderson with 250 shots three times a week, and Cath Cox with 150 shots a day, five days a week. Jane Altschwager shoots 100 goals a day and Sharelle McMahon puts up 100 goals four times a week. The important thing to note about this is that there is a fair amount of variation among top players as to how much shooting practice they do. Megan Anderson believes that the most important thing for her is to get her technique right and feel comfortable with her shot. In her words, 'each goaler should do what she feels comfortable with, rather than what everyone else is doing'.

The thing to remember is that the shots must be successful. So when Vicki Wilson shot 1200 goals a week, they were all successful (I hate to think how many shots she actually took to sink 1200). In order to ensure that shooting your training goals doesn't take you too long, you must have a sound shooting technique.

Shooting Technique

While each goaler has her own special way of sinking goals, it is good practice to have a basic technique to work from, particularly if you are having problems with your accuracy. Following are a few pointers from former Swifts goaler and Australian under-twenty-one representative Nerida Stewart.

To shoot from a basic stance, you will need to do the following:

❱ Place feet shoulder-width apart.

❱ Turn so feet and body are facing the post.

❱ Hold the ball primarily in your dominant hand (for example, if you are right-handed, hold the ball in your right hand, and if you are left-handed, hold the ball in your left hand), and rest the other hand on the side of the ball to help you balance it.

❱ Rest the ball on the fingers and upper part of the palm of your dominant hand (you should be able to fit a finger in between the middle of your palm and the ball). Make sure your thumb is not too far towards the front of the ball.

❱ Extend the dominant arm straight above your head, using the other arm to balance the ball.

❱ Drop the ball to the top of your head, not behind your head or in front of your face or chest.

❱ As you drop the ball, slightly bend your knees.

❱ To shoot, move the ball from just above your head back to the highest point above your head by extending your dominant arm and straightening your knees.

❱ Upon release, follow through with your dominant hand and flick your wrist to place a backspin on the ball. If you don't have enough power on the shot, it will hit the front of the ring and come back to you for the rebound. If you have too much power in the shot, there is a chance it will hit the opposite side of the ring and roll back into the goal.

❱ Release the ball at the highest point of the extension and come up slightly onto your toes.

When taking your shot, always remember to make your motion relaxed and smooth, not jerky. Your aim should be just above the front part of the ring and this is where your focus must be. If there is a defensive player blocking your view of this focal point, you can choose to step back or step to the side before you take your shot. If you do this, remember to keep your body balanced at all times. To ensure you are confident in taking this sort of shot, incorporate it into your shooting practice sessions, and always remember to vary the position you take the shot from. Another good way to prepare yourself for having the defender's arms over your shot is to have someone hold a broom over the ball as you shoot a few goals.

In your practice sessions you should also take shots when you are falling out of court. To make this more like a game situation, have someone throw you some high balls with you standing directly on the baseline. As you take the ball, immediately sight the ring and take a quick shot. Your technique won't always be pretty when taking these, especially if you are overbalancing. Nevertheless, it is worth practising them so that you know what is required to sink such a shot. If you get one of these goals during a game it will look pretty spectacular. It is, however, a last option. A safer option would be to turn and throw the ball back to one of the other players on court, and make a new lead to the ball. To do this, you will need one of the centre-court players or the other goaler to give you a call so that you know where to throw the ball. Another option is to spend a second trying to regain your balance, rather than falling out of court, but this means you will need to be able to get your shot away quicker than usual. To be prepared for each of these situations, try to practise them as part of your shooting sessions.

Rebounding

An important aspect of every shot is the rebound. A goaler should always be ready to follow their shot in, no matter how confident they may feel as they release the ball. The other goaler in the circle should also be working to find the prime rebounding position in case of a missed goal.

The best rebounding position is holding the space in front of your defender, preferably a step or two out from the post. It is important that you don't get caught directly under the ring, as the only rebound you will get there is the one that goes straight through. If your defender is trying to hold you away from the post, keep moving so that she has to keep repositioning herself. This may take her attention away from the shot just long enough to give you the jump on her if there is a rebound.

Top Tips

1. Don't ever assume that the shot is going to go through — follow every shot in for the rebound.

2. Keep the elbow of your dominant shooting arm as still as possible. While it will move forwards and backwards slightly when you bring the ball down and then up for the release of the shot, it should not move from side to side during the shooting motion. If this happens, your accuracy will be affected.

3. Try to get someone to defend you for your last few shots of practice. Get the defender to stand closer than three feet from you, and to vary the lean and jump on the shot. While this is happening, focus on your shot, which should help you block out what the defender is doing.

4. Practise shooting with loud music playing nearby, or with someone yelling at you. This will get you used to blocking out any distractions.

5. Closely watch the shooting technique of the various goalers in the Commonwealth Bank Trophy and see whose style you like (preferably someone with a high success rate) and try to model your shot on theirs. Take note of what they do in different shooting situations, and try to incorporate these techniques into your game.

Rebounding is always a hard aspect of the shot to judge — where will the ball go if the shot is unsuccessful? It is virtually impossible to know before the ball leaves the goaler's hands, so it is important that you are on your toes and ready to react to the ball as it comes off the ring. When attacking the ball off a rebound, your primary focus is to get to it with two hands and snatch it in. If you can only manage to get one hand to it, you can try to tip it into the space you are holding then keep jumping until the ball is safely in your hands. Alternatively, you can try to tap the ball to your other goaler.

A great way to improve your rebounding skills is to chase every shot you put up during a practice session, whether you think it's going in or not. When practising your rebounding skills as the goaler who is not taking the shot, face the goal in the position described above and have another person throw the ball up to the ring for you to react to. You can also position a chair or garbage bin near the ring to give you an obstacle to get around when you are going up for the rebound.

Shooting Drills

One thing that all of the goalers I spoke to recommended was that you practise shooting when you are slightly fatigued in order to replicate a game situation. Australian goaler Cath Cox sent me a great program that she incorporates into her warm-up. For her, shooting practice is a part of everyday training and is generally done thirty minutes before the rest of the team arrives for court-work sessions.

Cath starts her shooting session by doing twenty (successful) warm-up shots from all parts of the goal circle, after which she will stretch her arms for a couple of minutes and then take another twenty shots.

To ensure that she is practising shooting in a situation that replicates a game situation, Cath follows the initial warm-up with an active one that incorporates shooting at each end of the court when she's tired. You shouldn't start the secondary warm-up until you are in your natural rhythm, so if you didn't feel good during your warm-up shots, do some more until you start to feel comfortable. As Cath pointed out, if you are not comfortable with your shot while you are standing still, you certainly won't be when you are on the move!

The 'active' part of the active shooting warm-up is carried out in the same way as the team's normal active warm-up with certain shooting stations added after each activity.

Some examples of shooting stations are:

▶ A line of eight shots in a row, starting under the post and working out to the edge of the circle.

▶ Five to six shots taken in a semicircle around the ring from about halfway out.

▶ Five to six shots taken in a semicircle close to the edge of the circle.

▶ Take one long shot and one under the ring. Do this six times from different angles. You must pot both in a row before going on to the next pair.

▶ Twenty shots stepping forwards, backwards or sideways onto one foot before you shoot.

▶ Five shots taken as you are falling out of the court.

After completing the active warm-up, it's time to do so more specific drills incorporating movement and working with another goaler and feeder.

Once these drills have been completed, the rest of the team will have finished their warm-up, so everyone will be ready to start training together.

Drill One

The feeder starts with the ball in the centre circle. The goalers start midway between the transverse line and the top of the circle. The drill starts when the goalers split (i.e. when the front player makes a lead diagonally forward, and the back player reads off the movement of the front player to make a lead diagonally forward in the opposite direction). The feeder chooses one of the goalers and passes a straight pass to her. The player with the ball then turns and passes to the second goaler who is driving to the post. The second goaler takes the ball, steadies and shoots. Do this until each goaler has taken six shots.

Drill Two

The feeder starts with the ball at the top of the circle and a goaler starts just in front of the goal post. The goaler sprints to the side of the circle then back to the post to receive a pass and shoot. Do this five times.

The goaler then works for a couple of seconds at opening up space using dodges, rolls and so forth, takes a pass and shoots. Do this six times, then rest while the other goaler works.

Drill Three

The feeder starts at the top of the circle. Both goalers start in the circle, one on the front left-hand side of the circle, and the other on the back right-hand side. The goalers rotate around the circle clockwise or anticlockwise (it doesn't really matter as long as both are going in the same direction at the same time) and the feeder passes ten reaction passes. When one of the goalers chases the ball down, the other goaler moves to balance the circle up so that there is always one goaler on either side of the post (ensure that one is towards the top and the other towards the back). Whoever has the ball on the tenth pass shoots it. Do this for a couple of minutes.

For former Aussie goaler Jenny Borlase, shooting accuracy was something that she worked on from a young age. Jenny grew up in Cummins in South Australia, and from fifteen years of age onwards she would run one kilometre down to the local netball courts every day after school and shoot 100 goals. Back then, Jenny's shooting session didn't have any real pattern to it, other than trying to shoot as many in a row as possible, as quickly as possible. To try and cut her time down, she would chase the ball in for every rebound.

Like Cath Cox, Jenny was another goaler who found that getting her heart rate up before shooting was an effective way to practise. To do this, she would do some skipping, sit-ups or shuttle runs before shooting. She would also toss the ball up to herself, turn and shoot. The benefit of this is that it replicates what a goaler has to do in a game. While patterns such as shooting in a straight line or shooting a few goals in a row are good for technique, they aren't very game-like, so movement is the key to getting yourself used to shooting in game conditions. Yet there are definite benefits to be had from shooting a couple of patterns, as they help you settle into a rhythm. To this end, Jenny always finished her session by shooting ten goals in a row.

There is hope for those goalers who have neither the time nor the inclination to shoot a multitude of goals on a weekly basis. Interestingly, as Jenny matured as a netballer, she found that visualisation was just as beneficial as getting out there and popping in the goals. In Jenny's case, she actually found visualisation became more important to her than standing at a post, and eventually she only continued to put shots up on a regular basis out of habit. Visualisation involves imagining yourself taking shots from all around the circle in lots of different game situations — it goes without saying that they need to be successful shots! You also need to ensure that you are very confident in your shooting action and able to get quickly into a rhythm at the start of a game.

As well as accuracy, the other really important thing that most goalers who play for Australia have in common is that they have impressive netball brains. It is all very well to be able to pass, catch, run, jump and shoot — these are all skills that a great goaler must possess in abundance — but they won't take you all the way to top representative teams. To stand out from the rest you must be able to think several moves ahead. Your thought process can't be, 'How do I get the ball?', but rather, 'How do we set this up so that we can take a shot at a goal?'. These are very different things indeed. The first mind-set is really only thinking in terms of a single pass, whereas the second is thinking in terms of a whole play.

To help attacking players to think a couple of moves ahead, they must be encouraged to incorporate some set moves into their game. While these structured moves are very useful, goalers must be aware that no game situation is 100 per cent predictable: they must be able to adapt the moves to suit the situation.

Communication with your shooting partner and awareness of what she is doing are the keys to enabling you to adjust your set moves to a game situation. The relationship that you build with your partner will help to make you a winning combination. Working in conjunction with the other goaler during set moves enables you to achieve a prime position within the circle. While goalers can work independently during a game, when problems arise they need to be able to work together to combat them. One way to do this is through 'leads'.

Leads

Leads allow goalers to create movement to the ball without getting in each other's path or crowding the other attacking players in the goal third. Some goalers use leads only when they are getting in each other's way or both are stuck outside the circle, while others prefer to use them from the start to the finish of the game. An important thing to remember is to alternate your leads so the defenders can't work out your game plan.

There are four basic leads you can use. One goaler is nominated to call the lead during the game, and usually indicates the lead to her shooting partner by holding up one, two, three or four fingers. She can also call them verbally, although this should be done discreetly — you don't want the defenders to find out what you're up to! The leads generally work best when the ball is coming down from the defence end. Working leads off a centre pass is not always practical as the goal attack often has to take a centre pass.

When running leads it is essential that both goalers make their moves definite and precise so that there is no confusion among the other players on court as to who is leading for the ball. Remember that there must always be at least one goaler in, or driving into, the circle. The leads described below will help you achieve this, although they are not set in stone. If situations arise in a game where the play dictates that the goaler not on the lead to the ball should take a pass, then both goalers must adjust.

Lead One

The goal attack works the outside of the circle while the goal shooter remains inside.

Lead Two

The goal shooter drives out of the circle to the ball while the goal attack clears and drives into the circle.

Lead Three

The goal attack makes her attacking moves on the right side of the court, while the goal shooter takes the left side.

Lead Four

The sides in lead three are swapped, so the goal attack takes the left side and the goal shooter takes the right side of the court.

Leads provide goalers with a playing structure outside the circle. However, there are situations inside the circle in which pre-set moves can be used.

Screens

Screens are one example of a set of moves inside the circle. The underlying idea of the screen is to drag both goalers and their defenders together quickly, which creates confusion for the defenders as they figure out which player they will defend. Screens can get you out of sticky situations and look quite spectacular if executed well.

In setting up a screen there is no set position for the goal shooter or the goal attack, so we'll use the labels goaler one and goaler two. Goaler one's defender will be called defender one and goaler two's defender will be called defender two.

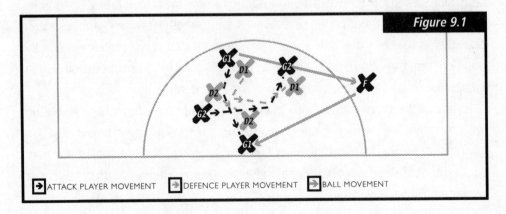

Figure 9.1

ATTACK PLAYER MOVEMENT   DEFENCE PLAYER MOVEMENT   BALL MOVEMENT

Goaler one stands near the top of the circle with the ball, and goaler two stands halfway between the post and the circle's edge towards the right or left back corner. A centre-court player, or 'feeder', is situated at the circle's edge on the opposite side of the circle to goaler two.

Goaler one passes the ball to the centre-court player and then runs towards defender two, placing her body between the defender and the feeder. At the same time, goaler two moves towards the feeder (both defence players will hopefully move with her). As goaler one gets close to defender two, goaler two will change the direction of her lead to the top of the circle and goaler one will open up to the ball with a lead along the baseline. As a result of the screen, defender one will have attempted to pick up goaler two as she leads to the top of the circle, leaving defender two behind goaler one as she opens to the ball. If defender one stays with goaler one, then this will leave goaler two free to take a ball near the top of the circle, as both defenders will be on goaler one. Figure 9.1 shows how the screen should be set up.

The screen has to be set up very quickly in order to confuse the defence. It is also important that goaler one does not have her back to the ball for longer than a second.

Another type of screen is called 'ridgy-didge'. This screen is used when there is a penalty pass on the outside edge of the circle. The name stems from an old children's television program. The children would call out: 'ridgy-didge' and hold out a hand with the thumb and pinky finger extended and remaining fingers curled in. If you were to do this with both your hands at once then place them alongside each other it creates a visualisation of how the screen looks.

The screen must be set up as soon as the penalty is given, and executed according to where the defence players position themselves. Remember, the ability to react to different situations is the distinguishing factor between a great goaler and an average one, and this screen is no different.

To set up the ridgy-didge, both goalers stand side by side facing the feeder, with the right foot of one goaler next to the left foot of the other goaler. The goalers' feet need to be as close as possible to each other so that there is no room for a defender to squeeze between them. There are three ways to execute a ridgy-didge:

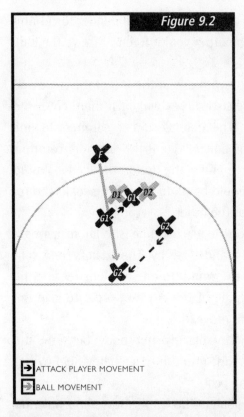

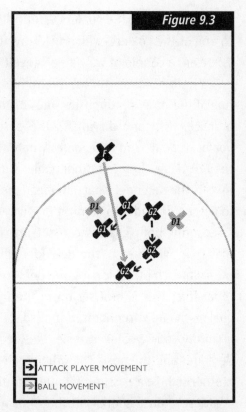

- If both defenders stand directly behind the goalers, it opens up either goaler to receive a straight ball from the feeder.
- If both defenders set up in front of the goalers, one goaler will move across and hold the space behind for the other goaler to step back and take a lob, as shown in Figure 9.2.
- If the defenders choose to stand to the side of each goaler, the goaler near the base of the circle turns her back to the defender closest to her and the goaler near the top of the circle turns her chest towards the defender at her side. This creates a screen for the goaler at the base to receive a lob as shown in Figure 9.3.

Remember, the positions of the body and feet must adjust immediately to where the defender is to enable a quick release of the ball to the space provided.

Ridgy-didge is a great screen to use when there are still two active defenders, but what if one of the defenders has been put out of play outside the goal circle? Ultimately, the goalers want to force the remaining defender to commit to one of the goalers, which will leave the other goaler free to receive the ball. There are a couple of ways to achieve this.

Firstly, the goalers can set themselves up with one at the top of the circle and one at the base, on opposite sides of the circle. They will each then move into a space, with one driving to the post. The defence either commits to one goaler or floats and anticipates where the ball will go. If the defender commits to one goaler, then the other goaler is free and is the option the feeder should take. If the defender floats, the feeder should baulk to one of the goalers to try to get the defender to commit one way or the other.

Secondly, both goalers can set up close to each other (similar to a ridgy-didge), in which case, the defender will stand close by. The goalers then split off from each other, forcing the defence to commit to one of them, leaving the other free. This is best set up in the middle of the circle in order to give the goalers the maximum amount of space to move into.

Thirdly, one goaler can set a screen by placing her body between the defender and the post. The other goaler runs into the space being held by her partner to take a pass, preferably near the post.

Variety is an essential attribute for a goaler. The more moves you have up your sleeve to beat the defence, the easier your game will become. The roll, as described in the chapter on basic skills, is a move that can be incorporated into your game in many situations. It is a great move to use when you have a defence who tends to overplay you or enjoys going for the first ball every time.

When a goaler performs a roll, the best area to begin is around the inside edge of the circle on the side that the ball is on.

Step One

Using the leg closest to the centre of the court, make a decent step forward towards the ball, shifting your weight to this foot. This initial step should make the defence think you will be making a lead out to the ball. Take the step just as the feeder receives the ball so that the feeder will not think you are making a straight lead and throw it to you. (If this does occur, the ball will either go out over the baseline or into the defender's hands.)

Step Two

Pivot on your leading foot and shift your body weight to what was your back foot. If leading to the left turn your body anticlockwise to face the post (turning clockwise if leading to your right) and sprint towards the post, watching the ball the whole time. Make sure that as you roll, you turn your head quickly so as not to lose sight of the ball for long.

Step Three

The feeder throws you a straight or slightly high ball as you move towards the post.

Step Four

Shoot from under the post!

The roll can be used all over the court and is definitely a move that needs to be incorporated into training drills. If you are having trouble getting the footwork right, place a cone out in front of you on an angle to give you a point to make the first step towards. Always start with a passive defence when learning the roll. There is nothing more frustrating than trying out something new at training and having a defender who knows exactly what you are doing. When you are comfortable with the move, try it during a training game to test if the defence can easily read what you are trying to do. If this is a success, the next stop to try it out is the GAME!

Top Tips

1. *Screens can be set up anywhere in the circle, or even outside the circle. Experiment in setting screens up in different places. The basic concept is for one goaler to run close enough to the other goaler for her to pick up the first goaler's defender and stop that defender from having a go at the ball.*
2. *Don't panic if you are not in a position to get the ball — you may be in a position to set your goaling partner up to get it.*

Chapter 10

Centre Court

Centre-court players are traditionally the quiet achievers on the netball court. They don't seek glory by shooting goals, nor do they attract attention by taking lots of rebounds. No, their job is to help the defenders defend and give the goalers the ball so they can shoot.

Despite the fact that they tend to go about their business quietly, centre-court players are incredibly busy people on the netball court. A centre must be competent at both attacking and defending, and must be fit enough to be doing one or the other for most of the game. A wing attack must possess both speed and an acute sense of timing. It is her job to set up the play in the forward line and deliver the ball to the goalers, and at the same time, read and react to whatever moves they put on.

Two of the best centre-court players were Carissa Tombs and Shelley O'Donnell, both of whom played for Australia in the 1991, 1995 and 1999 World Championship finals. They complemented each other perfectly because Carissa acted as the smooth link between the attack line and the defence line, while Shelley worked intensely and in short bursts of speed to direct traffic in the forward line.

The beauty of this combination was that although Carissa and Shelley had very different playing styles, they could both copy each other's tricks. While Shelley was renowned for her lightning passing, Carissa would occasionally thread a magic pass through several sets of hands to send the ball to the goaler under the post. While Carissa was an equally good defender as she was an attacker, Shelley could also take a mid-court intercept, which wing attacks generally don't do. This had an unsettling effect on the opposition, as it was difficult to predict what trick each player might pull out next.

Shelley wasn't the only great wing attack of recent times. Before Shelley O'Donnell there was Sue Kenny. Sue was the vice-captain of the Australian team (from 1989 to 1992) and a great controller of the play. The best way to describe the way she played would be to say that she had the ball on a string. Her pass selection was almost always spot on, and her ability to see and sum up her options in an instant was nothing short of amazing.

Marianne McCormick (née Murphy) was another talented centre-court player who was as tough and as fast as I have ever seen. Marianne played for Australia at the 1995 World Championships, and the only thing that stopped her playing in the grand final against South Africa was the fact that she played in the same team as Carissa and Shelley, two other great players. If Marianne had been born in any other country, she would have been the star of the show! As it was, her tenacity and 'no fear' attitude saw her as a star in my club team, Ku-ring-gai, and Sydney Cenovis (the precursor of the Sydney Swifts) for many years.

New Zealand's Sandra Edge was by far the most skilful centre-court player I have played against on the international court. I only played against one New Zealand team with her in it and for that I am grateful. She had a wicked look-away pass (which would just about fool her own team-mates), great speed and impressive endurance.

An impressive array of skills is required to be a good centre-court player. The necessary attributes are speed — as well as a quick 'turn of speed' — an acute sense of timing, vision, good pass selection and good decision-making skills. Tenacity is also highly desirable.

Speed

A good centre-court player needs to be able to carry out each of the basic attacking movements set out in the chapter on basic skills. She must be able to do these at varying speeds, as well as possessing good acceleration and a quick 'turn of speed'.

It is important for all centre-court players to be able to accelerate quickly from a standing start, but it's imperative for the wing attack at a centre pass. A wing attack needs to be able to accelerate at top speed to move away from the wing defence as the umpire blows the whistle for the start of play.

To help you do this if you are playing wing attack, it may help to start a little way behind the transverse line. That way, you can start making some preliminary movements, such as a dodge or double dodge, before the umpire blows her whistle. This will help to get your feet moving before you make your lead for the centre pass, as well as putting the wing defence off-balance at a crucial time. If you are a couple of steps back from the transverse line, you can do all of this without worrying about going offside before the umpire blows the whistle for the centre pass.

Centre-court players should practise their speed off the mark by pitter-pattering behind the transverse line and getting someone to blow a whistle. When the whistle blows, the player makes a straight lead over the transverse line to receive a pass from another player standing in the centre circle. Once the player has mastered this, she can then put in some preliminary movements such as dodging or double dodging before the whistle is blown and she drives over the transverse line to receive a pass. Next, place a cone somewhere between the transverse line and the centre circle and, starting behind the transverse line, get the player to drive hard to the cone on the whistle. Once the player gets to the cone, she must push off one foot and make a lead in another direction to receive the ball from the player in the centre circle. Finally, a defender can be added to make it even harder for the wing attack.

As well as being quick off the mark, a centre-court player must have a good 'turn of speed'. The term 'turn of speed' is used when a player goes from running at a moderate pace to top speed in a short amount of time, or vice versa. This is an important skill for a centre-court player, as it is impossible to run at top speed for a full game, particularly if you are playing centre! It is also important because as a centre-court player you will not receive every second pass, but you must be available for these passes in case you are needed. You must be able to follow the play at a moderate speed, and be able to accelerate quickly towards the ball. This is when turn of speed is crucial, as you have to break away from the defending player to receive a clear pass.

The best way to practise this skill is to simply run around inside the court at any angle and get someone to call 'go', which signals you to go from a jog to a sprint. When you hear 'stop', you go back to a jog. The sprint should only last for two to five seconds. You should also practise receiving a pass while sprinting and then stopping dead, passing, and moving off in another direction.

Spatial Awareness

Another important skill a centre-court player must master is the ability to know where she is in relation to the rest of the court, especially the edge of the circle, without having to look. The reason for this is when the player is feeding to a goaler, it is best to feed from the edge of the circle so the feeder's vision is not blocked by a defender. This will help a centre-court player to make a safe pass to the goalers. There will be many occasions when a centre-court player will be able to feed the goalers away from the edge of the circle, but it is preferable that she tries to get as close to the circle as possible. This way, after the pass, she will be ready to gather up any taps or be ready for a pass from a goaler trying to reposition herself in the circle.

The best way to practise landing on or close to the edge of the circle is to start at the transverse line, sprint towards the circle and stop as close to the edge of the circle as possible without going offside. You should practise stopping on both one foot and two. Once you have mastered this skill, do it without looking down until after you land. See how long it takes before you don't go offside! This drill will teach you to be aware of the circle's edge without having to continually glance down at your feet. The next step is to sprint towards the circle, stop and balance without going offside, then sidestep around the edge of the circle without looking down. Finally, add a pass, so you have to drive to the circle and catch the ball on the edge without going offside, or catch a pass while sidestepping around the circle's edge.

Top Tips

If you catch the ball on the edge of the circle and you feel as if you are going to fall offside, you can lean on the ball inside the circle, regain your balance and dispose of the ball. You will not be offside as long as only the ball is touching the ground — if you put your hand down inside the circle, you will be.

As well as getting the ball to the goalers, it is the job of the centre-court player to provide calming or encouraging words to the goalers. Ask them what you can say to help them shoot — generally something like 'steady' or 'breathe' will do. Alternatively, if they don't want to hear anything, remember to be quiet!

Pass Selection

A good centre-court player must possess sound ball skills. If you want to play in these positions, you will need to master each of the basic passes, and know when to employ each type to ensure that the ball reaches the intended recipient — most often a goaler in the circle. It is a fact of a centre-court player's life that some of your passes will get intercepted. The trick is to make it happen as little as possible and keep the defenders guessing. You also need to make sure when you are feeding in to a goaler that you deliver a pass which will allow them a higher-percentage shot at goal. In other words, it is your responsibility to get them as close to the post as possible. The skill of pass selection is one that will improve as your game matures.

The type of pass you select will depend upon a number of factors. Firstly, and most importantly, you must decipher what sort of pass is going to clear the hands of the player defending you, as well as those of the player defending your goaler. To clear the ball past the defender directly in front of you, you will need to look where she has her hands. If her hands are directly up in the air, you need to pass down low, so a bounce pass, or a shoulder pass kept reasonably low are safe options. If her hands are out to the side or down low, then a lob or an overhead pass will do the trick. To move your defender's hands, you can also try a baulk. This movement should be sharp and used sparingly.

To get the ball past the defender covering your goaler, you will need to read your goaler's body language. For example, if the defender is standing in front of your goaler, then as a feeder, you can read that the space is behind your goaler. If the goaler has enough space behind her, and the other goaler and defender aren't in that space, the obvious pass selection would be a lob into the space that the goaler is holding behind her.

If, on the other hand, you have a goaler who is holding space with her defender behind her, then your pass selection would be to drop a small bounce pass, or a direct straight pass right into her stomach. Which pass you choose will depend on the preferences of the goaler. Just like any player on the court, a goaler has her strengths and weaknesses. You should communicate with your goaler to find out which pass she prefers at the time. As a general rule though, a bounce pass is much harder to intercept than a straight pass.

What to do if the goaler's defender is moving? If the defender is moving around a holding player, you will need to get her to commit to one direction. A baulk is enough to do this. You can baulk as if to throw a bounce pass and then, as the defender comes around, throw a lob. The goaler can also continually reposition her feet as the defender moves so that she is always showing you the space to throw the ball into.

When you are throwing the ball to a goaler on the move, you will need to think about where you want her to end up. If she is driving towards you and has shaken off her defender, you need to get the ball to her straightaway so she can take the ball and move on to her next option. If you delay the pass, she will only end up further away from the circle, giving her more ground to cover to get back to a shooting position. When throwing this pass, or indeed any pass, to a player on the move, you must throw the ball ahead of the intended recipient. You need to aim to throw the ball to a spot in front of the moving player that allows her to move onto the ball without altering her speed greatly. If you pass the ball to where the attacking player is at the time you release the ball, the player will have moved past that spot by the time the ball gets there. This means that the ball will either miss the attacking player, which may result in a turnover, or, if the player has to slow down or stop to catch the pass, there is the risk that her defender can catch up and take an intercept.

If your goaler is undefended, then you need to take advantage of the situation and get her as close to the post as possible. You should think about putting a high ball close to the post for her to run onto. A word of caution here — the higher the pass, the more time it spends in the air, and the more chance a defender has of getting under it to take an intercept.

The final thing you will need to think about in your selection of pass is the whereabouts of any other defenders. It is pretty easy to find the players defending you and the goaler, but you have to keep your eye out for a third defender. This is particularly important if you throw a ball to a player running away from you. As a goal keeper, I like nothing better than a goaler or a centre-court player running backwards blindly to receive a nice, long, floaty pass. It presents a great opportunity to take a spectacular intercept! The simple way to avoid this is to make sure you look behind the player you are throwing to.

As well as choosing the right pass, at times you will also need to choose the right player. As a general rule, there should always be at least two players making a lead to the player with the ball. If this is the case, then it is best to choose the easier, shorter option, particularly at the start of a game. If you are well into the game and you are in a position to take risks with the ball, then do so — but don't forget that if you take a risk with the ball then you have to be prepared to accept the consequences if it doesn't come off! Experience has also taught me that if a game is close then always, *always* take the easier, safer option.

If you have two goalers giving you clear options to the ball and you have to make a split-second decision as to who would be the better option, you can make your decision based on the shooting position each goaler is in. In other words, you are better off giving it to the player closest to the post. If the positions of the goalers are fairly even and one of the goalers has a higher goal percentage than the other, then the better option is probably that goaler. Having said this however, it is important that you don't pass only to the player with the higher goal averages, as you need to ensure that both of the goalers are firing — if you don't give a goaler the opportunity to take shots it is a bit difficult for her to find her rhythm if she is struggling.

Vision

All players must be aware of what is happening around them. To do this, players must use their visual skills to take in the total situation rather than focus purely on one particular area. As a centre-court player, this vision is vital when you are organising the attacking play and, in particular, feeding your goalers. You must be able to see the moves of each of your goalers, as well as what the defensive players are doing to counteract those moves. You must also be able to see what your other centre-court colleague is doing on the outside of the circle. In other words, you must be able to take in everything that is going on and make your decisions based on what you see happening.

You must also use your vision to work in and around the goalers. It is pretty tempting in a game to run straight towards the ball, or to get to the edge of the circle as fast as possible. Unfortunately, this is not always the best option. You need to use your vision to take in where each of the players is on the court and then decide where to move to create some balance. For example, the top of the circle always seems to be the place that gets cluttered first. If you see a goaler making a move to the top of the circle, see if there is a better place for you to go, either in the pocket (the section outside the circle closest to the baseline) or back towards the transverse line.

The best way to practise taking in the commotion of a netball court and making the best decisions is to do ball-work drills with flashcards. Flashcards are cardboard squares approximately 15cm x 15cm in several different colours. Using any drill you like, get a person to stand behind each thrower holding a set of flashcards. As the worker catches the ball, a card is flashed to the side or above the head of the thrower. The worker must call out the colour of the card without stopping the drill. Players should be familiar with the drill before adding the flashcards. Don't be surprised if you find that you stop once you catch the ball and think about the colour you have seen on the flashcard before you call it out. This is something you don't want to do so really concentrate on catching the ball, sighting and calling the flashcard, and moving on with the drill. The better you get at the exercise, the better your on-court vision will be. Once you are comfortable with the flashcards in a drill situation, the next step is to set up a half-court situation in training and have people stationed on the sidelines and baseline and get players to call the colours as they are flashed.

Top Tips

1. *A centre or wing attack should never plant herself on the circle once she reaches the edge. It is best to keep moving on, off and around the circle to give you and your goalers space and to be an option to receive a pass.*

2. *Try not to get caught deep in the pocket. It is pretty hard to get a pass to there as you have little room to move. If this happens, come off the edge of the circle and try to move towards the top.*

Timing

When do you make a move towards all of the action and when do you stay away? This is a difficult skill to master — it just takes practice and familiarisation with your team. As a centre-court player, you are the link between the defensive end of the court and the goalers, so what you do between these two ends is vital in getting the ball down the court. As general rule, the defenders (with some help from the centre) should bring the ball from the defensive baseline through to the centre of the court. As a centre, you should not get involved in the play too often prior to this. You should move into a space, ready to take a pass if you are needed at the last moment. One of the best players when it came to being a true link between defence and attack was Carissa Tombs — she had a great ability to stay out of the way until she was needed, when she would be in the right place at the right time.

How much a centre will be involved in bringing the ball down the court will also depend on how good her goal defence and wing defence are at attacking. Kath Harby is a strong attacking player, as well as being a top defender, so whether she is playing for the Thunderbirds or Australia, she assumes a leading role in bringing the ball down the court, which means that whoever is playing centre essentially stays out of her way until needed!

Once the ball reaches the centre of the court, the wing attack and goal attack should become the two options to take the ball into the attacking third. The centre will then read the moves of these two players and make an attacking lead. Once the ball is into the attack line, the best move for the centre to make is directly to the edge of the circle — make sure that you check to see where the wing attack is to ensure that you do not end up on top of each other.

Things are different for a wing attack, as you will need to assume the role of rallying the troops at your end of the court. You will need to use your speed to shake your defender, and your court sense to set up plays and set the tone for the attack line. Don't be afraid to be assertive in your role, although be aware of the space being used by your goal attack and goal shooter. Finally, don't be tempted to get caught too far up the court when the ball comes towards you.

As a rule of thumb, try to start behind the transverse line and don't make a move until the ball has come past the centre circle. This will give your defenders plenty of room to bring the ball to you, and you won't waste energy getting caught a long way from the circle.

It is hard to set hard and fast rules about when you should become involved in the play and when you should stay out of the way. As a general rule, if you are making several moves and not being used then you should not be there. Get out of that space, and get further down the court to be used at a later stage. As a centre-court player, don't feel that by clearing down the side of the court you aren't doing anything — you are doing more good by giving your team-mates plenty of space to work in.

Chapter 11

Defending

While there is plenty of pressure on goalers to perform, and centre-courters are the quiet achievers, I can safely say that defenders are the unsung heroes of the netball court. I can hear all of the protests of the centre-courters and goalers as they read this, but those defenders who go into battle week in and week out will know what I am saying is true!

When I was first handed the goal-keeper bib I nearly cried. 'What a useless position,' I thought. 'All I get to do is chase the goal shooter around and get penalised by the umpires.' For some games, that is still a reasonably accurate assessment of how I spend my time, but I soon discovered that I loved playing goal keeper. I love trying to anticipate where the ball is going to go. There is no better feeling than taking a flying intercept and then seeing your team-mates race the ball down-court to score.

Occasionally, I get let out for a bit of a gallop in goal defence, which generally scares my team-mates so much they forget how to play, so it is not an option that any of my coaches often take. However, when they do, I enjoy playing goal defence. I like being let out of my little area to chase the goal attack around and have a go at feeding our goal circle from the centre third. I must say, though, that I am always happy to return to the relative safety of goal keeper. For some reason, I never get a turn at wing defence!

Australia has a great history of tough defenders who worked their insides out to get hold of the ball for their team and who terrorised opposition goalers. As a youngster, I didn't really get a chance to watch many of the great defenders because netball was not televised back then (that makes me sound old, I know!). When I was selected in the NSW under-seventeen team, we had a practice match against the NSW Open Team — well, it was a practice match for us and a warm-up for them! Even though I knew the names of the players, it was the first time I had seen many of these women play. One player stood out for me on that day. The NSW Open Team goal keeper was Keeley Devery, and I watched every move she made and committed it to memory.

From that day on, Keeley was my hero. She was an impressively skilful defender who made her opponent work incredibly hard to get the ball, yet she was such a clean player. Not once did I see her hold on to an opponent's arm or uniform. Every intercept she got was the result of hard work. She also had an incredible defence of the shot, so even if her player did manage to get the ball, she faced a tough assignment having a shot at goal. And if the shot missed, then the opposition could kiss possession goodbye, because very few players could out-rebound Keeley.

To top it off, my hero was a great person. I loved being in a team with her because she was always nattering away and making us all laugh. But she was also passionate about the game. I remember a team talk with the NSW Open Team in Darwin at the National Championships in 1993. We were attempting to win New South Wales's seventh straight national title. Things weren't looking so good, as we had gone down to South Australia and struggled against Victoria and Queensland in the rounds. There was a perception among our team that the umpires were letting a lot of physical play go, and in the round match against South Australia, we didn't cope very well with the rough and tumble of the match.

In the team meeting before the grand final, Keeley, as our vice-captain, let it rip, and told everyone in no uncertain terms that if our opposition became physical, we were to stand up to it and become stronger because of it. She left us in no doubt as to her opinion of our 'heart muscles' and worked herself into some good, old-fashioned tears of anger and frustration. It worked, and we won the final by two goals. It was one of the best pre-match talks I have ever heard.

So, all in all, Keeley was not a bad role model to have! She was skilful and uncompromising. She also made a great duo with Sharon Finnan, whose physical and mental toughness saw her represent Australia on numerous occasions. Sharon never left the side of her opponent. There is no such thing as an easy catch with her. And while she doesn't pick off an enormous number of intercepts, the amount of pressure she places on an opponent often creates turnovers further down the court.

I have also felt very privileged to play alongside defenders who will be remembered as greats. When I first broke into the Australian starting seven, I played alongside the captain of the team, Michelle Fielke (now den Dekker). Michelle was one of the fittest netball players I have ever seen. No goal attack could outrun her. She was another player who worked the ground in front of her attacker, and never let them take an easy pass.

Since Michelle's retirement, Kath Harby has stamped her name on the Australian team's goal defence bib. Kath plays a very different game than Michelle did, in that she allows her goal attack more room to move. This allows the goal attack to take more uncontested passes, but it also frees Kath up to have a fly at the ball as it moves down the court. She is able to do this through an uncanny ability to read the play and an impressive turn of speed. She also has no fear, and her reasonably diminutive size in comparison to the 183-centimetre plus goalers we come up against in international competition does not impede her willingness to put her body — and the body of anyone else who gets in the way — on the line to get the ball. I really enjoy playing with Kath, although it is worth noting that while her anticipation is impressive when she is on my team, it is infuriating when I am playing in an opposition side!

Alison Williams is the defender I play most of my netball with, as she is the goal defence for my club team, the Sydney Swifts. Ali has developed from a too-short goal keeper into a tough goal defender. She has a great ability to read the play, and she is prepared to have a go at any ball that is floating around the goal circle. One of Ali's greatest strengths is her rebounding ability. If you watch her closely, you will see that she has an impressive vertical jump, and when she gets her hands on the ball she is incredibly strong when pulling it in to her body, so there is no chance of it getting knocked from her hands.

It would be remiss of me not to mention wing defenders here. Wing defence is a tough position to play well — turnovers don't come your way from a rebound, and the wing defender's movement is restricted by her inability to run into the circle. Add to this the fact that most wing attacks are very fast and suddenly it doesn't look like an appealing position — although try telling that to the players who have made this position their own.

The benchmark player for all wing defenders is Simone McKinnis. Simone played for Australia for over ten years, and in that time became one of the best defenders in the world. I was fortunate to play behind Simone in the Australian team for several years and I got to witness her great speed, extraordinary timing and tough attitude. Any ball that floated into the pocket was fodder for her, and the way she used her hands over the ball when it was in the attacker's hands saw her pick up a phenomenal number of intercepts. Peta Squire has stepped into the enormous shoes of Simone McKinnis in the Australian team and she is doing a terrific job of terrorising wing attacks the world over! I've spent a lot of time with the Swifts watching the exploits of Raegan Jackson as wing defence. She plays a vastly different game to Peta in that she grinds the wing attack into submission, rather than taking dazzling intercepts. Rae's strength as a player lies in her tenacity as a defender — the wing attack never gets a moment to rest — and her steady attack play when we make a turnover.

Australia does not have a mortgage on great defenders. On the international stage there have been some awesome defenders who have made — and in some cases are still making — life hard for our goalers. New Zealand netball fans still talk in hushed tones of the prodigious talent of goal defender Wai Taumaunu. Wai was the captain of the New Zealand team that went down to Australia by one goal in the final of the World Netball Championships in 1991, and she is still revered as one of the greatest players ever to wear the goal defence bib. Current New Zealand captain Bernice Mene has every chance of rivalling Wai Taumaunu as one of the greats of New Zealand netball. There have been many games when I have stood at the other end of the court and been impressed by her speed and agility. For a player as tall as Bernice, the way she moves around the court is nothing short of spectacular.

Oberon Pitterson from Jamaica, Amanda Burton from England and Leanna Du Ploy from South Africa are also some of the current crop of international players who make life hard for our goalers.

One thing that is evident from the way all of the players I have mentioned approach the game — every defender has her own unique style. Some are hard workers who wear their opponents down so turnovers come from opposition mistakes. Others concentrate less on the player they are marking and more on the passage of the ball, so they are more likely to take the spectacular intercepts that the crowds love.

There are also some distinctive styles of play between countries. Australia is known for our close marking of opposition players and a one-on-one style of play where we tend to stick with our designated opponent.

New Zealand, on the other hand, play a 'zone' defence where the players defend a space on the court rather than a particular player. This style of defence was adopted by our trans-Tasman neighbours in an effort to combat the speed of the Australian team in the centre court. It is a particularly effective method of defending because it slows us down and makes us look to second, and sometimes third, options when we are attacking. This style of defence does have a couple of weaknesses, however. Firstly, setting up a zone through the mid-court necessitates that both the wing defence and the goal defence stand in the centre third regardless of where their players are. This means that if our defensive players are able to bring the ball through the mid-court reasonably quickly, it frees up our wing attack and goal attack to have a free run to the circle with only the goal keeper to defend them and the goal shooter. Secondly, it is possible to draw the goal keeper out of the circle by baulking to the edge of the circle where the wing attack or centre might be running. This allows a clear pass in to the goal shooter. Despite these limitations, the zone defence is a potent tool that has given us plenty of problems in the past.

Jamaica tend to oscillate between the zone and one-on-one defence. They play an incredibly tight one-on-one game as the ball comes down the court, but they tend to drop into a zone defence as the ball gets closer to the goal circle. As the ball gets to the edge of the circle, it becomes a bit of a lottery as to whether they will split the circle, so that each defender defends a particular half of the circle, or whether they will revert to one-on-one. How they do it, I don't know, but they rarely get it wrong. The Jamaican style also relies heavily on their defenders' athleticism. Generally, their defenders aren't that tall, but they can jump!

One of the notable things about our games against Jamaica is the body clashes. The Jamaican defenders have an uncanny ability to get themselves under the attacking player, so when she tries to land, she finds that there is nothing to do but crash into her opponent and then onto the floor. This has resulted in some fairly heated matches between Jamaica and Australia. One game that comes to mind was during the 1999 World Netball Championship, when Jamaican wing defence Sharon Wiles was 'sin-binned' for five minutes for continually causing herself and our wing attack Shelley O'Donnell to get up close and personal with the floorboards.

The New Zealand press felt that Shelley was lucky not to be sent off with Wiles, but I believe that is an unfair assessment of what went on in the game. Shelley was not about to back down, and I don't believe she had to. She may have given some of her own back, but at the end of the day, she was being denied space to land and that is against the rules of netball.

In the remainder of this chapter, we will concentrate on the Australian style of defence and what skills need to be acquired to become proficient at it.

My personal approach to defending is that it is the defender's job to annoy the attacker. It might sound strange, but this is, in fact, the essence of defending. As defenders, we must annoy the attacker as much as possible without touching her. The way we do this is to move our feet to stop the attacker from going wherever she wants to go, to not let her catch the ball without also trying to catch it, and to not let her pass the ball or take a shot at goal without our hands being in the way. If that isn't annoying, then I don't know what is!

The other thing that is worth remembering is that your feet are the most important part of your body when you are defending. It is the speed of your feet that will get you to the ball when you are going for an intercept, and get you out of trouble when you are in a position where you may contact a player.

There are three components to defending, which every player, whether she is a goaler, centre-court player or defender, should be familiar with. These are:

▶ having a go at the intercept;

▶ if you miss the intercept, recovering to three feet away from the thrower and getting your hands over the ball; and

▶ after the attacking player passes the ball, working the ground to deny her the opportunity to run where she wants to go.

Having a Go at the Intercept

Essentially, there are three ways that you can get your hands on the ball through an intercept.

Firstly, you can attempt an intercept from the front-on defensive position. This is the best position to adopt when you are defending a player as you are placing yourself between the ball and your attacker, so in order to get the ball, your player has to get in front of you first. It is also the position least likely to get you into trouble with an umpire, as you are less likely to contact your opponent when you are going for the ball if you are in front of her.

Secondly, you can attempt an intercept from the side of the attacking player. This is a little risky, as you have to make it clear to the umpire as you go for the ball that you are not touching your opponent.

Thirdly, you can have a 'fly' at the ball. This is something that you might do if you are caught out of position and you see the ball travelling to another attacker and you think you might be able to get it. You can also fly at the ball if you are covering your opponent and you anticipate where the ball is going to go and you fly into the air to get the intercept. This particular method of defence, however, is fraught with danger. If you are successful then you look like a complete legend. If you miss the ball then you look like a complete fool. It is risky, but I have spent enough time looking like both to know that it is worth a go!

Let's take a closer look at how you can work on each method.

Front On

As a defensive player, take up your starting position in front of the attacking player and with your back to her. Do not stand directly in front of the attacking player because you will not be able to see where the attacker is. Rather, half of your body should be covering half of the attacker's body. If you are standing in front of the attacker and slightly to her right, the left side of your body should cover the right side of the attacker's body (and visa versa if you are standing slightly to the attacker's left). You then keep your head on the left side the whole time you are covering the attacker's movement.

The important points to remember when defending front-on are:

▶ Start so that half of your body is covering half of the attacker's body.

▶ As much as possible, try to keep your head on one side. If the attacker starts to dodge left and right, move your feet to keep up with her, rather than moving your head to find her. Swinging your head from side to side only results in you losing the attacking player completely, and takes your eyes away from where the ball is. If you find that you are swinging your head from side to side, try to imagine that there is an elastic band attaching your chin to the shoulder you are looking over. The elastic band will keep snapping your head back into place whenever you are tempted to move it!

▶ KEEP YOUR EYES UP! It is common for defenders to drop their eyes to the attacker's feet the moment the attacker starts moving. Don't do this — the ball very rarely gets thrown to your opponent's feet! You should start with your eyes looking at a point midway between the player you are defending and where the ball is. It sounds difficult, but the defender must know where the ball and her player are at all times. Also, if your eyes are down, there is every chance that a smart attacker will throw the ball straight over your head to your player. This only has to happen a couple of times in a game to make you very wary of dropping your eyes.

▶ Be careful of 'feeling' for the player behind you. If you lose your attacker, it is tempting to feel behind you with your hands to try and find where she is. If the umpire catches you, it is a pretty soft penalty to give away.

Once the attacker dodges, she will often take a couple of steps towards the ball. If you have managed to cover the dodge, commit really hard to having a go at the intercept. The worst piece of advice I ever got was that when you are playing goal keeper, you should only follow the goal shooter to the edge of the circle — once she is past the circle let her go and pick her up on the way back in. NO WAY! Don't let your player take an easy pass. Even if you don't have a go at the intercept, go with her. Some players are prone to drop the ball if they know you are right behind them.

A good drill for defending front on is to pair up players. One works as the attacker and the other as the defender. The players should find a line to work on, with the attacker starting behind the line and the defender starting in front of the line, facing the attacker. Both players start as close to the line as possible without crossing it, and try to stay close throughout. The attacker then dodges left and right behind the line, moving about one metre each side of the starting point. The attacker can dodge, run, touch the ground, jump — essentially, she can do whatever movement she wants as long as it is just behind the line. The defender has to follow the attacker and mimic her movements. Once both players have had a turn, they do the drill again, but this time the defender turns around and uses her front-on defensive position. Now the defender has to follow the attacker while keeping her eyes up so that she can see what is going on in front of her.

The next phase is to add a player who will act as a thrower. The attacker and defender do the same thing as before (with the defender facing the thrower), but this time the thrower passes a straight chest pass to the attacker every three to four seconds. Because the aim of the drill is to practise intercepts, it doesn't matter if the defender is in front of the attacker when it is time to throw the ball. The final phase is to allow the attacker to move forwards over the line to take the ball. This movement is the most difficult to defend, so it may be worth restricting the attacker to a straight drive to start off with, and gradually allowing her to dodge and roll.

Side On

Side-on or 'T' defence is a useful alternative to the front-on defensive position. It is useful when a defender is getting pasted by an attacker who is dodging every time to take the ball, or when an attacker is using only one side of the court. This is because the side-on defence allows the defender to dictate to the attacker which space is available to her. Occasionally, I like to use this method on goal shooters, as they have a tendency to drive out to the left-hand side of the court. The reason they do this is that the goal attack tends to work on the right side, so a goal shooter is likely to balance this by working on the left side of the court. To deny a goal shooter the left-hand side of the court is potentially very annoying to her as it can really put off her timing — and the timing of her team-mates who are used to her running to a particular area.

Side-on defence is sometimes called 'T' defence because the defender's body in the starting position makes a 'T' shape with the attacker's body — if you can imagine the attacker's body being the vertical line of the 'T' and the defender's body being the horizontal line. This is only a guide, however, as the middle of the defender's body should actually be slightly forward of the attacker's shoulder.

Basically, the defender sets up on the side of the attacker, making sure that she allows enough space between herself and the attacker for the umpire to see that there is no contact between the players. When the defender goes for the ball, she must do so with her front arm. Obviously, there will be occasions when the defender will be able to go for the ball with both hands but as a rule, side-on defence necessitates the defender using her front, or outside, hand to tap the ball — either down so she can regather it or to one of her team-mates. Using the back hand requires the back shoulder, which is closest to the attacking player, to come forward, which will almost always result in the defender's shoulder coming into contact with the attacking player.

There is a very simple drill to practise this. Players are split into groups of three with one ball between them. Each player has a turn at being the attacker, the defender and the thrower. The thrower sets up about three metres in front of the attacker. The defender sets up in her side-on defensive position, and starts pitter-pattering her feet. The thrower throws a chest pass to the attacker, who only takes half a step towards the ball (the attacker should be passive so the defender has plenty of practice taking intercepts). The defender takes a step forward with her front foot to try and tap the ball down with her outside hand. She then moves her feet forward and around the attacker to collect the ball. The next phase is to throw a variety of passes so that the defender has to react to each pass. Finally, the attacking player is allowed to have a strong go at the ball as well.

The drill can be further developed so that the attacker uses her body to hold space in front of, or to the side of, the defender. The defender then has to move her feet to move away from the body of the attacker and around the side to have a go at the ball. The advantage of coming off the body is that if the attacking player is pushing into the defender, the umpire is more readily able to see the attacker causing the contact than if the defender stays in contact with the attacker's body.

This is particularly important if the defender is caught behind her player. There is little point having a go at the intercept from behind, as umpires will only let that go once in a blue moon. Rather, if the defender is caught behind her attacker, she will need to move her feet so that she can have a go at the intercept from the side or in front. If the defender cannot move her feet to go for the intercept from either of these positions, she would be better off conceding the first ball to her player and getting back three feet to put some pressure over the pass.

Having a Fly

This approach to getting an intercept can pay enormous dividends, or it can leave you feeling pretty useless! I must admit, I really enjoy taking these intercepts, and it is getting a flying intercept that makes all of the hard work worthwhile.

I like to settle into the game a little before I attempt to charge out of the circle to have a fly at the ball. That way, I can get a feel for the way the ball is coming down the court and where each of the attacking players tends to run. It is generally best to have a go at a longer pass to a player who is running backwards in your direction. As a goal keeper, that tends to be the centre or wing attack, and it is generally when they are running into one of the pockets on either side of the circle. The passes I have a go at also tend to be ones with a bit of 'float' in them. It is pretty difficult to cleanly intercept a straight, hard pass when you have to cover a fair bit of distance to get there.

Often, it is this skill that distinguishes a good defender from a competent defender. This is because a flying intercept tends to be the one thing that a defender can do that is really out of the ordinary. Done at the right time, it can lift your team and even inspire a victory. Each of the defenders in the Australian team has this ability, and if you watch Kath Harby, Liz Taverner and Peta Squire, you will see that they are often able to pull off spectacular intercepts that really lift the rest of the team. It is not only defenders who can take these intercepts. Rebecca Sanders and Megan Anderson are both players who can pull off valuable intercepts in the mid-court by anticipating where the ball is going to go.

A fly at the ball takes a little planning, a little luck and a lot of daring. Firstly, you need to be able to read the play and anticipate where the ball is going to be thrown. Some players are able to do this instinctively, while others have to work to see where the opportunities for having a go at the ball arise. Secondly, you need to have the confidence to go for the intercept. Once you see the opportunity to intercept, you have to commit wholeheartedly to it. If you have a half-hearted attempt, you are likely to be left standing in no-man's-land, neither taking the intercept nor defending your player. Thirdly, you need to let your team-mates know that you are coming. Don't forget that your team-mates in front of you are often blind to what is happening behind them. A simple call of 'mine' or 'got it' should be enough to warn your team-mates that you are coming.

For players who have trouble reading the play and anticipating when to have a fly at the ball, there are some fairly simple drills that can be done to help them recognise the situation when it arises in a game. These drills are also good for players who can easily read the play to fine-tune their skills.

Set up a thrower, attacker and defender as they would start for the front-on defensive drill described earlier. (Although for this drill, the attacker stands still to start with.) A second attacker is added about three metres away from the thrower, as shown in Figure 11.1. The thrower starts the drill by facing away from the defender, tossing the ball in the air and catching it, and turning to face the defender. As the thrower turns, the second attacker runs in a straight line down the court, as indicated by the arrow. The thrower then throws a high, 'floaty' pass to the attacker. The defender must leave the first attacker and have a fly at the pass to the second attacking player.

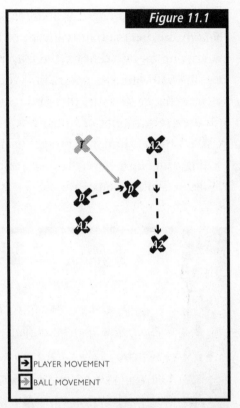

Figure 11.1

PLAYER MOVEMENT

BALL MOVEMENT

Once the defender is confident with having a fly at a high ball, the thrower can then choose to throw either a high pass, or, if the defender moves too early, she can throw a straight pass to the first attacker. The next phase is to allow the first attacker to dodge (although her movements should be confined to a reasonably small area), so that the defender has to concentrate on covering her player as well as knowing where the second attacker is and when she can safely leave her player.

Hands over

Defending over the ball at three feet is an important and underrated component of defending. It is as important as going for an intercept — if you can try for an intercept when your player is receiving the ball, there is no reason why you can't go for an intercept as your player is disposing of the ball. Even if you don't get an intercept or a tip as your player passes the ball, you may set up an intercept for the player behind you. If you are putting pressure over the ball with your hands, or if you are in the attacker's line of vision, there is every chance that she will not throw a good pass to one of her team-mates.

There are a couple of important things to remember when defending the pass. Firstly, it is important to get back three feet before putting your arms up. Putting arms up before the feet are back is a common mistake and it often results in a soft penalty.

Top Tips

1. When you are defending, always start off pitter-pattering as the ball comes towards you. This way, you will be ready to follow the attacker.
2. Always keep your eyes up. Very little interesting action takes place around your feet.
3. Don't be tempted to pull an attacker's arm away from the ball or hold onto her uniform. Not only it is against the rules and against the spirit of the game, it also displays a distinct lack of skill — attempt to get the ball fairly and cleanly.
4. Learn when to go for the intercept and when to pull out. A good defender knows when she should back away from the contest so that she doesn't give away a penalty.
5. When you are training, if you get a hand to the ball and tip it away, chase it down hard. This will prepare you for game situations when you will need to chase the ball. Standing and watching the ball bounce away at training isn't very good match practice.

Secondly, you should not have to look down to know whether you are three feet (ninety centimetres) away from the thrower. You should practise stepping back three feet until you can do it automatically. This is a very easy thing to practise. Just make two marks on the ground three feet apart. Stand on one mark and, without looking down, step backwards to the other mark. Once you have stepped backwards, look down and see how close you are to the mark. Keep doing this until you are confident that each time you step back you are at least three feet away from where you started. If you are small, you may need to take a couple of small steps backwards, rather than one big step. It also worth remembering that you are better off taking a too-big step rather than a too-small one. It is best to be back more than three feet and not be as effective in your defence rather than be back less than three feet and be penalised.

Finally, you should be balanced as you are defending the pass. At my clinics, I find that when I ask players to sprint to a line, step back three feet and put their hands up, most players get right up on their toes with their legs locked and their arms straight in the air. While this position takes up plenty of space in front of the attacker, it doesn't really impede her throwing. When defending a pass, players should be on the balls of their feet with their feet shoulder-width apart. Their knees and elbows should be slightly bent and their fingers outstretched. The advantage of this position is that it allows the player to jump as the attacking player passes, so she can have a go at the intercept. It also means that the defender is ready to work the ground to stop the attacker from going where she wants to go once she has passed the ball.

This stance also tricks the attacking player into thinking that she has enough space to pass the ball. Because the defender's arms and knees are bent, she is, in effect, taking up less space than she would if she was on her toes with her legs and arms stretched as far as they could go. When the defender stands at full stretch, the attacker can see exactly where the space is available to throw the pass around the defender. When the defender stands with her legs and arms slightly bent, the attacker thinks she has more space and will generally only throw the ball as far around the defender as is necessary to get the pass away. If the defender is standing with her arms and legs slightly bent, she has the option of stretching out into the space that the ball is being passed into.

Top Tips

1. Mix up defending the pass by putting your hands either directly over the ball or in the air in the attacking player's line of vision. This will keep some doubt in the attacker's mind as to where the best space is to pass around you.

2. Sometimes stand directly in front of the attacker, and sometimes stand more towards her throwing arm. Standing towards the attacker's throwing arm will often cause her to pass across her body, and therefore across the court, which is an easier angle for one of your team-mates behind you to go for an intercept.

Working the Ground

Working the ground is the least enjoyable aspect of defence. There is no escaping the fact that it is pure hard work. It takes an awful lot of discipline to keep moving your feet so that you are constantly in the path of the attacker. This particular skill has never been one of my strong points, and if you watch carefully, you will see that during a game I sometimes have a tendency to just turn and run with my player back to the circle. If you can avoid the pitfall of just turning and running, you will be well on your way to being a good defender.

The reason we work the ground is because it upsets the attacking player's timing and rhythm. If we let the attacking player run wherever she wants to go, she will easily find the space to receive the ball, and find team-mates to pass the ball to. If, on the other hand, we are constantly making her change direction, her timing will be out, which will force her team-mates to look for other options, which, in turn, affects the timing of the whole team. Working the ground has the added effect of making the attacking player work hard to get the ball, as she may have to make several leads before she receives it. If we can make her work so hard that she becomes fatigued, then she may make a bad decision with her pass, or she may be too busy trying to breathe to think about her shooting technique.

To work the ground, a player must start in a reasonably upright position with her arms by her sides. She should start on the balls of her feet with her feet shoulder-width apart and her knees slightly bent. As the attacking player moves to her left or right to avoid a collision with the defender in front of her, the defender's movement will be lateral. This means that it will be either a sidestep or a sidewards run. It doesn't really matter what the movement is as long as it is fast enough to cut off the attacking player's intended path. The name for the movement is a 'defensive slide', which is essentially a backwards zigzag done with a sidestepping motion. The zigzag is not enormous, just a couple of steps either side.

Top Tips

1. *Remember to keep your eyes up! Just because the attacker is trying to get past you doesn't mean that she can't be thrown the ball.*

2. *Don't be tempted to stick your elbows or knees out, or drop your shoulder, in an attempt to stop your opponent from running past you.*

3. *The key to working the ground effectively is taking little steps.*

4. *Try to direct your opponent away from where the action is. Often this will mean steering her towards the sideline. As well as taking your opponent out of the play, it will put you between her and the ball, which is always a good position to be in!*

Players should practise the defensive slide in isolation first. They can do this by standing on one side of the court and doing a defensive slide to the other side. Next, add an attacking player whose job is to jog slowly in a zigzag across the court, with the defender's job being to follow her closely. The attacking player should then build up speed so that after a while, the defender is able to work the ground at full speed.

It is worth remembering that it is very difficult to do this outside of a game situation, and it is likely that the defender will only be able to hold up the attacking player for a few seconds. Don't despair! A delay of two or three seconds is sufficient to upset the attacking player's timing.

Each of the three components of defending can be put together in a fairly simple exercise. Put players into groups of three and where possible, try to have one goaler, one centre-court player and one defender. The centre-court player can start with the ball up near the transverse line, with the goaler and defender in the circle. The defender sets up either front on or side on to the goaler. The goaler starts by making a lead out of the circle and receiving a pass from the thrower. The defender attempts to intercept this pass. If she misses, she must recover and put pressure over the pass back to the thrower, who runs down to the top of the circle to receive the ball. Once the goaler has passed the ball back to the thrower, she runs back into the circle to receive a second pass from the thrower. The defender must work the ground and stop the goaler from driving into the circle, and then try to intercept the second pass.

This drill can be done by all players, so, for example, if a goaler was to become the defensive player in the drill, you might set it up so that she is defending the goal defence on a throw-in. A centre-court player might also do the drill from a defensive throw-in or centre pass.

Defending the Shot

Defending the shot is the last line of defence your team can offer before a goal is scored, so it is imperative that circle defenders spend plenty of time working on this. All defenders have a particular method of defending the shot, and if you watch the Commonwealth Bank Trophy, you will see some different styles. While we all try to mix up what we do on each shot, there are some things that each defender will do more than others. Sarah Sutter has a great reach, so more often than not, she will lean right over the shot. Janine Ilitch tended to jump, although her approach was different as she often jumped twice before the goaler released the ball. Liz Taverner mostly leans over the ball with one hand, often swapping arms midway through her lean. Depending who I am playing against, I prefer to jump on the shot, although, unlike Janine, I tend to hold off for as long as possible and jump just the once.

There is no 'right' way to defend the shot, although there are a couple of wrong ways. In defending the shot, you have to be careful not to be seen to be intimidating the goaler — that is, your efforts have to be directed towards the ball, rather than waving your hand around in front of the goaler's face. You must also take care not to break the three-foot distance between yourself and the goaler. So, it is probably not worth jumping twice unless you are sure that your first jump will be straight up in the air, rather than forward. If you do jump and land within three feet of the goaler, or if you overbalance, you should try to get out of her way. To do this, you simply need to move to the side of the goaler.

In order to be a nuisance to the goaler, you will need to be able to mix up your defence of the shot. In the first quarter of the game, try each method and take note of which one seems to work. Once you have figured out what puts the goaler off, start doing it more and more. Try not to fall into the trap of doing the same thing all the time though, as you need to keep your opponent guessing about what you are going to do next.

There are two ways of defending the shot. The first is the lean, and the second is the jump. There are a couple of variations within each that will give you plenty of variety in your defence.

Leaning

The most important skill in leaning over the shot is balance. To be effective, you will need to be able to balance up on your toes for about four seconds (I reckon that's how long it takes most goalers to shoot!). To practise this, simply set aside a couple of minutes at the end of training and find a line. Walk along the line, stopping to balance on one foot for four or five seconds every couple of steps. Gradually increase the amount of time you are balancing, and then start to put your arm out, as if you are defending a goaler. You will need to be able to lean equally well on either foot, so it is worth practising balancing on each.

The most basic lean is the one-armed lean. This is simply a matter of leaning over the ball with the arm of the same leg you are balancing on. This is the lean that will give you the most reach over the ball. If you are leaning on your right leg, then your left leg should be off the ground to help you balance. If your right arm is up over the ball, then your left arm should be outstretched behind you, also helping you balance. Your left hand should be ready to have a go at the ball if the goaler passes off to her team-mate in the circle. One little trick that is quite useful is, if you are leaning over the ball with your left hand, for example, and your right hand is outstretched behind you, have your fellow circle defender hold on to your hand or even your skirt to stop you from overbalancing. This will allow you to balance longer and it will also help you lean further over the ball. While this is useful, it should only be done on a reasonably close shot, as holding on to your skirt or hand will take some of your team-mate's attention away from her player.

An alternative to leaning with one hand is leaning with two. This takes up more space over the ball, although you won't be able to lean as far over the ball as you can with one hand. To ensure you get as far over the ball as possible, you should still try and get up on one leg. The only times it is worth staying on both feet are if you are having trouble balancing, or if you think the goaler may pass the ball rather than take the shot, in which case it is important that you are ready to cover the next pass.

The one-armed lean may be modified by swapping arms midway through the lean and concentrating on leaning over the shooting arm. Swapping arms will help you balance, and it is possible that the movement will also distract the goaler from her focus on the goal ring. Leaning over the shooting arm is perfectly legal, as long as you don't touch it and you make an effort to defend the ball. The advantage of this is that it may put the goaler off slightly by taking up her space to shoot.

Another variation is an 'inside lean'. This is where you lean over the ball with the opposite arm to the leg you are balancing on. For example, if you balance on your left leg, you would defend the shot with your right hand. Your right leg is bent up to take up the space between you and the goaler, and your left arm is generally behind you to help you balance. In order to stay balanced, you will need to remain reasonably upright and stretch your hand over the ball. The advantage of this type of lean is that where you are defending a player who likes to step in on her shot, it allows you to take up the space she would normally step into.

Jumping

Jumping on the shot should be fairly basic. It is simply a matter of jumping and trying to hit the ball, right? Wrong! It is slightly more complicated than that. Most goalers shoot at different times — some are quick, but most take the full three seconds and some hold on as long as possible. There are also differing styles and release heights to contend with.

To get an idea of your opponents' shooting styles, spend a little bit of time during the warm-up watching them shoot. This will give you an indication of how long they take to shoot and where they release the ball from, which, in turn, will help you decide on when and where to jump. It will also help you to start formulating what your early strategy should be. If the release of the ball is quick, you know that you will have to either put your arm up to lean or jump fairly quickly. If the goaler's release is low, you may want to start the game by jumping on the shot, as you stand a better chance of tipping the ball that way.

Once you have an idea of the timing and height for your jump, you will then have to contend with the fact that goalers will baulk in an attempt to get you out of the way before they release the ball. Watching the goalers' warm-up will give away their 'natural' body movement when they shoot. This will help you know when a goaler is baulking and when she is shooting. Very few goalers go through the whole shooting motion when they baulk, so if you are familiar with their shooting motion, you will know when they are going to baulk and when they are shooting for real.

There are a couple of different ways to jump on the shot. You can either lean and then jump, or crouch and jump, or jump a couple of times. The advantage of leaning and then jumping is that you don't give the goaler a clear view of the goal ring because you are always in her face. The disadvantage is that you can't get as much height because jumping from a lean doesn't allow you to generate much power from your legs.

Jumping a couple of times performs a similar function to leaning and then jumping, as you tend to be in the goaler's face as you keep jumping. It also allows you to generate plenty of power with the second jump.

The danger of this, as I said earlier, is the risk of obstructing on your second jump. Unless you can be sure that you are going to land on or behind your original position, it isn't worth doing. Even if you allow more than three feet in your starting position, so that you can land closer after your first jump, you may be penalised, as umpires often see your starting position and presume that is three feet, so if you move closer from that original starting position you may be seen to be obstructing — even if you aren't!

My preferred method is crouching and then jumping. This doesn't mean that I squat right down before I jump, but I tend to bend my knees slightly so I am ready to jump the moment the ball is released. Occasionally, I put one of my hands up to let the goaler know I am there, although it would be overrating it to call it a 'lean'. Putting one hand up also gives me some leverage on my jump. I crouch slightly with my left hand in the air and as I jump, I swing my left arm back and my right arm forward to try and tip the shot. Doing this helps me to gain more height on the jump, and swinging my right arm through ensures that my movement is towards the ball, rather than straight up in the air.

Top Tips

1. Make sure that when you lean your arm is as far over the ball as it can go. Similarly, when you jump, aim for where you think the goaler will release the ball from, rather than straight up in the air.
2. You will get further over the ball if you push your hips up and out as you lean.
3. Stretch your fingers out as far as you can on your lean — you will be surprised how much closer to the ball you might get.
4. You can mix up a jump and a lean on the same shot. This is done by crouching as if to jump at the shot, and if the goaler baulks, go into a lean. This may put some doubt in the goaler's mind, as her baulk is intended to get rid of you completely by getting you to jump early.
5. You are not going to tip every shot you jump at. Your aim should be to put doubt in the goaler's mind. If you can tip a shot early in a game, it may well be that you have dented the goaler's confidence enough to put her off her shots just by threatening to jump.

Rebounding

The defender's job doesn't finish with the defence of the shot. If defending the shot is the last line of defence, then getting a rebound is the first line of attack.

Rebounding is hard work. When there are four bodies pushing to get a good position and four sets of hands grasping for the ball, it is not easy to pull the ball in. Defenders can increase their chances of getting the ball by preparing for the rebound before the shot is taken. The defender who is not defending the shot needs to be thinking about her rebound position early. This means that as the goaler is shooting, the second defender should be keeping her opponent as far away from the ring as possible.

The player who is defending the shot also needs to be thinking about her rebounding position. This is why it is imperative that her timing is spot-on if she decides to have a jump at the shot. If the defender jumps early, she runs the risk of losing her rebounding position, as she has to get out of the goaler's way in order to avoid giving away a penalty.

The best rebounding position is between the goaler and the post. If you are defending the shot, you will already be in this position — the important thing is to keep it. The way to keep it is to move immediately to take up your rebounding position once the shot is taken. You only have a split second to do this while the goaler is completing her follow through. There are a couple of ways of doing this. If you are leaning over the shot, you should step as close to the goaler as you can, without touching her, the moment she releases the ball. As you step into the rebound space, you should turn to face the post so that the goaler is behind you and you can see the path of the ball.

If, for example, you are leaning over the shot with your right arm and balancing on your right leg, the best way to take up a good rebound position is to step forward onto your left foot so that it is roughly in front of the goaler's left foot. You then swing around to place your right foot in front of the goaler's right foot. You should finish so that your feet are slightly wider than shoulder-width apart — remember, you want to take up plenty of space so that the goaler can't get around you. You may need to move your feet to keep the goaler behind you, but be careful of pushing back into her and giving away a penalty.

Similarly, on the jump, you should aim to time your jump so that you land after the goaler has released the ball. This way, you can turn in the air and land in a good rebounding position. The important thing to keep in mind is, if you are defending a goaler who steps in as she shoots, you will have to allow for this in your landing. If you aim to land close to the goaler's starting position and she steps in, then you are likely to land on the goaler and give away the penalty.

Once you have a good position that you have managed to maintain, it is important to get up strongly into the air for the ball if it rebounds anywhere near you. This means going up with two hands, and once they are on the ball, pulling it in. As I mentioned earlier, if you watch Alison Williams play, she does exactly this. Ali's rebounding is so strong that once she is anywhere near the ball, it is likely to end up in her hands. Sharelle McMahon is another player who rebounds incredibly well. Even though most defenders tower over her, she is not scared to get up and pull the ball in with two hands.

If you are playing against a tall goaler, you are being out-rebounded, or you are not in a good rebounding position, the other option is to attempt to tap the ball either to yourself or to a team-mate. When I get caught behind a goaler, I find that I am better off trying to tap the ball backwards to myself or to a team-mate rather than risk pushing the goaler and giving away a penalty by going up with two hands.

Tapping is a particularly useful ploy when you are playing against tall goalers. Even though I stand at just under 183 centimetres, on the international court I tend to be on the short side. This means that often I will not be able to get two hands on the ball in a rebound situation. The way Kath Harby and I get around this is that I go up for the rebound with just one hand — which allows me to reach further — and try to tap the ball to my goal defence. She gives me a call as I go up to let me know where she is, and I try and aim it at her voice.

Another thing to remember about a rebounding situation is there will generally be plenty of pushing and shoving. To get used to taking the ball under that sort of physical stress, you can practise rebounding against a wall. You will need a reasonably high wall and another player to throw the ball. Get her to throw the ball up high against the wall. As she does, step into a rebounding position, and as you go for the ball get her to give you a gentle shove in the back. Don't shove too hard, or you will end up face-planting the wall or, worse still, hurting your back. The push should be just enough so that you have to adjust your body position to be able to get up to the ball.

Top Tips

1. Practise your rebounding every chance you get. If you are doing a drill at training where the goalers get to shoot, take the opportunity to practise your rebounding.

2. Try not to get caught directly under the ring when a shot is being taken. The only rebound you will get in this situation is one that comes straight through the goal ring.

3. Always try to take up a rebounding position — don't be content to turn and follow the ball.

4. Don't ever assume that the goaler will get the ball in — even the best goalers miss shots next to the goal post.

Defending the High Ball

One question that young players ask me is how should they defend a tall goaler. Often it is because they have come up against a particular goaler who is tall enough to stand in the circle and receive lobs from her team-mates. The problem arises when the goaler in question is much taller than the defender, with the defender feeling that, short of chopping the goaler's legs off, there is very little she can do.

This is actually a problem that I face almost every time I walk onto the court for Australia! New Zealand, England, Jamaica and South Africa all have goalers that make me feel tiny! Each of these countries boasts goalers who stand 190 centimetres or taller, so, at a touch under 183 centimetres, I generally look like a little kid trying to match it with the big girls. The most lethal of these goalers is Irene van Dyk, who recently left South Africa to play for New Zealand. Not only does she stand at 190 centimetres, but she is a goal keeper's nightmare because she can run, jump, pass, catch and, worst of all, shoot regularly at 90 per cent accuracy. I first played against Irene in 1995 in a test series against South Africa prior to the 1995 World Championships. The first time I played against her, I felt as if all I had done for sixty minutes was jump as high as I could only to come down empty-handed. So you can imagine what my nerves were doing to me before I came up against her in the World Netball Championships final a couple of months later.

Fortunately, we had spent plenty of time analysing both Irene and the players around her. Coach Jill McIntosh had come up with a game plan that was designed to starve Irene of the ball by disrupting the feed into her. We knew that in a one-on-one situation, I could not out-jump Irene if the feed was well placed. Our game plan was to put the feed off to give me a chance of getting a hand to it. The plan worked beautifully. Wing defence Simone McKinnis and centre Carissa Tombs had their work cut out — their job was to get their hands up and over the player with the ball in order to get her to drop the pass short. This would allow goal defence Michelle Den Dekker and I to get our hands to some of the feeds. So while Michelle and I received most of the credit because we were the ones taking the intercepts, it was the hard work of Simone and Carissa — who spent most of their time sprinting from one player to another and defending the pass — that set up the win.

The other thing that I had to do in that game was continually adjust my starting position on Irene. As the ball came down the court, I had to ensure that I was moving around so that the feeders never really had a clear idea of where the space was to pass the ball into. This is a really difficult thing to do, as it means that there are times when you are not really sure where the goaler is and what space she is holding. It is worth doing, though, because not only does it put doubt in the feeder's mind, but it also gives you enough space to move your feet and have a go at the ball.

The Australian team has not really changed our approach to defending tall goalers over time. The strategy has been successful so far — mainly because it is simple. It relies on disrupting the feed to the goaler, rather than on the goal keeper attempting to out-jump her.

The final thing to remember when playing against a tall goaler is that as a goal defence or a goal keeper, you are not going to get every ball that comes in. I get pretty despondent when I see the ball go over my head for most of the match. I have to keep reminding myself that I am really only going to get my hands on the misfeeds, so I have to be patient and wait for them to happen — if they don't happen, I can always blame the centre-court players in front of me!

Top Tips

1. Take lots of little steps around your player so that you can readjust quickly when she sets up a hold.

2. For particularly high lobs, or particularly tall players, go up with one hand and try to tap the ball to one of your team-mates. Get them to call to you as you jump so that you know where to tap it.

3. If you are having trouble, get your fellow circle defender to drop back and help you. If you do this, be sure to watch for the goal attack if she runs into the circle, as one of you will need to pick her up once she is inside the circle.

Chapter 12

Fitness for Netball

For some people, playing netball is one way of getting fit and keeping fit — and that is fantastic!

If, on the other hand, you want to improve your netball by improving your general fitness and strength levels, then this chapter is for you. There are several different components to netball fitness: endurance, speed, agility and strength. All of these can be worked on during the pre-season and maintained throughout the year so your body is ready for, and continues to cope with, the rigours of a netball season.

I often get asked by young players about what extra training they can do to improve their game. It is my firm belief that a player really doesn't have to do an enormous amount of extra training until she reaches about fifteen or sixteen years old, or maybe earlier if she starts to move up in the representative ranks. Until players reach this point, they should be getting enough cross-training playing a couple of different sports to have to worry about too much extra training — particularly endurance training. Nevertheless, players can always benefit from a little bit of extra work.

The Australian Netball Team and all of the Commonwealth Bank Trophy teams structure their year into different phases. The first phase of the season is the pre-season, and this is generally a couple of months long. The pre-season is broken up into a couple of stages. The first stage concentrates on building a solid endurance and general strength base. A typical training week during this stage usually involves two or three endurance sessions. These are generally either a forty-minute run, swim or cycle at low to medium intensity with the aim of developing a sound aerobic base. This stage would include at least one general speed session, which can be covered by cross-training. A game of tennis, squash, touch football or basketball should fit the bill. The training week is topped off with two or three strength sessions. These strength sessions are done in a gym and they focus on abdominal stability, arm and leg strength, and flexibility, using our bodyweight or light weights to gain extra strength.

The second stage of the pre-season sees us move into training sessions that are far more netball specific. We continue to do two or three endurance sessions per week, although they now move to a higher intensity. To do this, the actual time spent on the session becomes shorter, but the intensity of the workout increases. Endurance sessions during this stage essentially involve working at medium intensity as a base level and moving into high-intensity work for short bursts. This is achieved by way of fartlek training. The name fartlek always makes me laugh — until I have to do it. Believe me, it is hard work.

An example of a fartlek session is to run for thirty minutes, with the thirty minutes being broken up into ten three-minute blocks. These blocks are then split up so that we run at low to medium intensity for two minutes, and then at high intensity for one minute. As the pre-season progresses, the actual time spent on each block of high-intensity work decreases, while the number of high-intensity blocks increases. For example, in the same thirty-minute period we would move from ten blocks of three minutes to thirty blocks of one minute, where we run at low to medium intensity for forty seconds and at high intensity for twenty seconds.

The second stage of the pre-season also sees us move into a more specific strength-training phase. We move from a focus on stability and flexibility to a focus on general strength. To do this, we use light weights with high repetition, while maintaining the stability and flexibility developed earlier in the pre-season. We also move from relying on playing other sports to maintain our speed to specific sprint programs which have us doing longer sprints — up to fifty metres — and concentrating on technique. This stage also sees us move into court training with our Commonwealth Bank Trophy teams. For the Swifts, this involves two on-court sessions a week.

The second phase of our conditioning program is the period between the pre-season and the start of season, which is the pre-competition phase. This phase has us move into high-intensity endurance sessions, weights sessions that focus on power, and sprints that are short and sharp. Agility is included as a major component of this phase, if it has not already been introduced during the pre-season phase. Agility is a valuable component of our training because it is important not only to be able to run fast, but also to be able to change direction at speed and sprint off in a new direction.

Once the season starts, the number of sessions that we do per week drops off and the focus becomes quality in shorter sessions. This is the third phase of the strength and conditioning program, which is the competition phase. By this stage, most of our strength and fitness training is just about complete and we concentrate on maintaining our strength and endurance levels throughout the year. The only aspects of our overall conditioning that can really be improved upon once competition starts are speed and agility. This is because these two things will improve with more match play, as well as the fact that on-court training during the competition phase focuses quite heavily on short, sharp movements.

The fourth and final phase of netball training is the off-season. This is an absolutely vital stage for us because during this time we get to recharge our batteries and freshen up for the next season of netball. I remember as a youngster being really disappointed when netball season finished, and I couldn't understand why I couldn't play all year round. Now there are so many different competitions that not only can you play netball all year round, but you can play it every night of the week as well as weekends if you want! Things have changed for me since I was a young netball player, however, and now I enjoy the off-season. Top-level competition really takes it out of me both physically and mentally, so I need a couple of months at the end of the year to completely switch off. During this time, I generally try to concentrate on getting some work done and reacquainting myself with my family and friends. I also try to do something completely different, like yoga, swimming — and even getting married. Well, I did do that in an off-season a couple of years ago!

While all netball teams should structure their training so that it includes some pre-season fitness, it does not need to be anywhere near as intense as the Australian Netball Team program I outlined above. On the contrary, a reasonably good level of fitness can be attained simply by playing a couple of different sports during the week or getting some other regular exercise. Nevertheless, some sort of conditioning work should be undertaken, either as a team or individually, to ensure that the players are ready for the season ahead.

As a cautionary comment, if you are coaching a team and you plan to set a fitness program, you should carry out a pre-season physical screening to ensure that each player in your team is able to complete the program. A sports physician or sports physiotherapist will be able to do this.

If you are planning to undertake a personal fitness program in the off-season, you should also see a sports physician or sports physiotherapist to get a clearance to do so. You should also ensure that you have a good pair of running shoes which have been selected to suit your foot type. Some sports stores employ qualified podiatrists to help customers select shoes that best suit their feet. While good running shoes are expensive, they are worth having if they will prevent injury and enhance your training regime.

One other point to make is that if you plan to run as part of your conditioning program, then do so on grass or at a running track. It is important that you avoid running on hard surfaces like bitumen or concrete as much as possible, as the jarring effects of running on a hard surface can lead to injuries.

You should ensure that each conditioning session is preceded by a thorough warm-up and followed by a warm-down. There is no point in working hard to get fit if you are failing to prevent injury. To to this, ensure that you listen to your body. If any exercise or drill starts to hurt, then stop. If you do injure yourself, have it attended to straightaway, and if you start to feel tired or lack energy, then give yourself a break until you are feeling ready to go again.

Once you are ready to start, you need a strength and conditioning plan. As I said earlier, the program of the Australian team is far more than you will need to do. It is, however, a guide to the phases of a team's training through the season. In order to get the most out of your pre-season, you will need to start at least two, or preferably three, months before the season starts. As a general rule, you should work hard in training for three weeks in a row, with the fourth week being a lighter 'rest' week.

Your pre-season training should be made up of either endurance, strength and stability, or speed and endurance sessions.

Top Tips

1. *If you don't have a sports watch to time your fartlek, you can use telegraph poles. If you are running next to a road (remember to run on the grass next to the footpath — never, ever run on the road), run at a lower intensity for several telegraph poles and then sprint between two poles. Gradually reduce the number of poles you pass as you are resting. Trees can serve the same purpose.*

2. *For the sake of your personal safety, don't run late at night and try to use several different routes — don't run the same route at the same time on the same day each week.*

3. *A good alternative to plain running or swimming is running in a pool. A twenty-five metre pool with waist-deep water is perfect, and it makes for variety in your training routine.*

4. *If you suffer leg or back injury during the year, swimming is an excellent way to keep fit while you are out of action. Consult your physiotherapist for a program.*

Endurance

The first month of pre-season training should be used to build your aerobic fitness by either running, swimming, cycling, or rowing on an ergometer three to four times a week. By the end of the first month you should be aiming to work aerobically for about thirty (and no more than forty) minutes at low intensity. Don't fall into the trap of trying to work too hard too early. Even if you are able to do thirty to forty minutes of fitness work really easily, it is important that your early work is done at a low intensity. This is because you need to build up your aerobic rather than your anaerobic fitness during this period. In plain English, this means that you need to establish a base whereby you get your body used to working at a lower intensity for long periods, so that you can perform more efficiently at higher intensities later in the pre-season. If you ignore your base aerobic fitness and move too quickly into anaerobic work, where you are working at high intensities, you will not be able to work as long and as hard as you would if you had a strong aerobic base.

Don't be discouraged if you find it too difficult in the first couple of weeks to do an aerobic session for the full thirty minutes. Even now, I struggle to run for thirty minutes at the start of the pre-season, and I can guarantee that I couldn't run out of sight on a dark night when I was fifteen. If this is the case, start by working at a low intensity for as long as you can. Then aim to increase the time by about ten per cent each week — except for your rest week, where you should reduce the time you are working by about twenty-five per cent. Eventually, you will be able to work quite solidly for thirty minutes. It is also worth remembering that the first pre-season conditioning program you undertake will be the hardest. I have found that each pre-season gets a little easier than the one before. I think that this is because each year I lift my base level of fitness that one extra notch, so I am starting each year slightly fitter than I was the year before.

The second month should see you start to increase your intensity during your endurance sessions. To do this, you can either run, swim or ride faster for the same amount of time, or you can start to introduce some fartlek training for one or two of your endurance sessions. One way of getting yourself to go faster is to try to do your normal route or program in less time than you usually take, or to cover more distance in the same amount of time.

Fartlek training can be introduced slowly by working for twenty minutes and alternating between low and high intensity. This can be done by running at low intensity for two minutes, and then high intensity for one minute. As this gets easier, gradually increase the amount of time you are working to thirty or forty minutes. You can also start to move from low-intensity work in the down periods to medium intensity, so you are working for two minutes at medium intensity and one minute at high intensity.

In the third month, you can move into even higher intensity fartlek training two to three times a week, while keeping one endurance session as a longer, slower session. The work-to-rest ratio in the fartlek should now be changed so that the time spent in each of these periods is reduced. Once again, start the month by dropping the total session time to about twenty minutes, but increase the amount and frequency of high-intensity work. For example, you could work at a low to medium intensity for forty seconds and at a high intensity for twenty seconds. This can gradually be increased so that you work at a low to medium intensity for twenty-five seconds and a high intensity for fifteen seconds.

So as you can see, the aim of pre-season endurance training is to establish a base level of aerobic endurance and build that into a high level of anaerobic fitness. This is achieved by starting off with long, slow sessions and gradually moving to some high-intensity work coupled with increasingly shorter rest periods. The relevance of the training becomes apparent when you consider that a game of netball is made up of short, intense periods of work, broken up by rest periods.

During the season, your endurance can be maintained by doing one twenty- or thirty-minute session per week. However, this is desirable rather than absolutely necessary. I find that I rarely get time to do an endurance session a week during the season. One thing that makes me giggle is when the Australian team conditioning program calls for a 'recovery run' which can be carried out the day after the game. As far as I am concerned, there is no such thing! A run for me is always hard work, so I can think of better ways to recover from a game.

Strength and Stability

Pre-season training needs to include plenty of strength and stability work. You should focus on core stability, all-round flexibility and strength work using bodyweight to build strength. If you are not yet eighteen, or if you have not finished growing, you should steer clear of a heavy weights program. Until that age, stability and flexibility are the most important things to work on.

Once you hit eighteen, stop growing or start moving up the representative ladder, then you can begin to add weights to your strength program. I didn't embark on a weights program until I went to the Australian Institute of Sport when I was eighteen years old. When you are ready to start a weights program, you should go to your local gym and get one tailored to your specific needs by a trained instructor. Ensure that you explain to them that you want a program that establishes a general strength base and moves into a power phase just before the season starts. Plyometrics can also be introduced during the power phase. (Plyometrics are exercises that use your own bodyweight to increase the strength in your legs, such as tuck jumps, bounding and forward two-legged hops. These exercises replicate in short bursts certain movements that you would do in a game. You might, for example, do three sets of eight tuck jumps with one minute of rest time in between sets.) The program should be tailored so that it doesn't aggravate any injuries you may have; and have your technique checked by the instructor, as heavy weights combined with poor technique will lead to injury.

Until you are ready to tackle a weights program, the strength component of your conditioning training can be made up of stability exercises, bodyweight exercises and flexibility work. This should be done two to three times per week during the pre-season. When the season starts, you can drop it back to one or two sessions per week.

These sessions should be structured so that there is an adequate warm-up and then equal amounts of time spent on each of strength, stability and flexibility. For example, your session could be structured as follows.

▶ A fifteen-minute warm-up (include some sort of activity that gets your heart rate up, for example try running or skipping, and do ten minutes of stretching)

▶ A twenty-minute circuit (an example of a circuit is described on pages 156–159)

▶ Twenty minutes of stability exercises (choose some from those on pages 160–161 or use a Swiss ball)

▶ Twenty minutes of stretching (make sure you stretch each major muscle group, holding each stretch for thirty seconds, and go through each stretch twice)

The beauty of this sort of session is that the only equipment you really need is a towel or, if you want to go really upmarket, a gym mat! Things like Swiss balls or hand weights are optional extras.

Strength and stability exercises can be chosen from the examples set out on pages 156–159, or you can make up your own. The flexibility exercises can be chosen from those in the chapter on warming up.

The best way to develop your strength using bodyweight is through a circuit. I recommend doing a twenty-minute circuit. A simple circuit consists of five exercises, which you perform four times each, allowing forty-five seconds for each exercise and a fifteen-second rest between each one. Alternatively, you can do a ten-exercise circuit and go through each exercise twice.

It doesn't really matter how many exercises you choose, as long as you work each muscle group. Broadly speaking, you need to ensure that there is at least one exercise for your abdominals (including your back), one for your arms (including your chest) and one for your legs.

The beauty of this sort of circuit is that it costs you nothing because you can do it in your own backyard. You can also tailor it to your fitness needs. As you become fitter and stronger, you can increase the work period and decrease the rest period so that you are working more and resting less.

Set out below are examples of exercises that can be incorporated into a strength circuit. To make it easier for you to structure your circuit using these exercises, I have split them into abdominals, legs and arms.

Abdominals (including back)

Sit-ups

Lie on your back with your knees bent and your feet flat on the floor. Keeping your arms straight, slowly sit up and touch your knees with your hands. Once you can do this comfortably, increase the difficulty by taking your elbows to your knees; crossing your arms over your chest while sitting up; and resting your hands against your forehead while sitting up.

Crunches

Tense your stomach and back muscles as you would for a stability exercise. Lie on your back with your legs bent and rest your feet on a bench so your shins are perpendicular to your thighs. Place your hands behind your head and, using your stomach muscles, lift your shoulders as far off the ground as possible, hold for a couple of seconds, and then lower them. Ensure that you don't 'pull' your head forward with your hands — to avoid this, try to keep your chin pointing to the roof.

Oblique crunches

Tense your stomach and back muscles as you would for a stability exercise. Lie on your back and hold your legs in the air with your knees bent at a 90° angle. Slowly move your left elbow towards your right knee. Repeat on the other side.

Ankle touches

Start as you would for a sit-up and lift your shoulders a couple of centimetres off the ground. Bending from the waist, move to the side to touch your left ankle with your left hand, then move across to the right to touch your right ankle with your right hand.

Side sit-ups

Start as you would for a sit-up, then drop your knees to one side so that the bottom knee is touching the ground. Slowly sit up as far as you can, hold and go back down.

Legs

Bodyweight squats

Start with your feet shoulder-width apart and your arms stretched straight out in front of your body. Bend your knees until they are at a 90° angle, keeping your feet flat on the ground. To increase the difficulty, a small weight can be held in each hand.

Single-leg squats

Follow the same procedure as a bodyweight squat but do it while balancing on one leg.

Heel raises

Start with your feet shoulder-width apart. Slowly rise up and balance on your toes, hold this position for a couple of seconds, and lower your heels back to the ground. To increase the degree of difficulty of this exercise, you can use a step: start with your toes on the edge of the step and your heels hanging down over the edge, and go into the heel raise from there.

Tuck jumps

Jump as high as you can. At the top of your jump, tuck your feet up under your body. Try to land on the balls of your feet to keep the landing light and to minimise the time you spend in contact with the ground. The moment you land, start the next jump.

Burpees

Do a tuck jump, then as you land, place both hands to the ground in front of your feet. Balancing on your fingers, quickly straighten your legs until you are balancing on your hands and toes, then quickly bring your legs back to your chest to straighten up and jump again.

Lunge walk

Start with your feet shoulder-width apart and lunge forward onto one foot. As you land, drop your back knee almost to the ground then push off the back leg and lunge forward. Keep going for ten metres.

Step-ups

You will need a strong bench or a very sturdy box about thirty centimetres high. Step up onto the bench or box with your left leg, then bring the right leg up to touch the top of the bench or box. Step off the bench or box right leg first, then bring the left leg down. Either alternate leading legs for each step-up, or lead with one leg for the first half of the time and the other leg for the second half.

Arms (including chest)

Push-ups

These can be done as half or full push-ups. For full push-ups, start on your hands and toes; for half push-ups, start on your hands and knees. Ensure that your body is in a straight line from your shoulders to your toes, or shoulders to your knees. To get the most out of the movement, lower your chest to as close to the ground as possible.

Chin-ups

Do these on a strong bar that can hold your bodyweight. Start with your palms facing towards your body and try to lift your body until your chin is above the bar. You may need to get someone to assist you by holding your legs and helping you up to the bar.

Bicep curls

Use hand weights or a couple of full drink bottles. Hold the weights down by your sides with your palms facing outwards. Keeping your elbows tucked in by your sides, slowly move one hand at a time up to your shoulders and back down.

Tricep curls

Using a single hand weight or drink bottle, hold the weight straight up above your head with your elbow straight. Slowly move the weight down to the back of your neck and straight up again. Make sure you do the exercise on both arms.

Bench dips

Use a strong bench or sturdy box and sit right on the edge of it. Place your palms on the edge of the bench or box with your fingers over the edge. Move your feet away from the bench or box and take your weight on your arms. Lift your bottom up and forward and slowly move it towards the ground. Once you are as far down as you can go, use your arms to lift yourself back up so that your bottom is in line with your hands. Increase the degree of difficulty by moving your feet further away from the box; and then by placing them up on a box of equal height to the box your hands are on.

These exercises are just some examples of strength exercises using your bodyweight or small hand weights. For variety, you can add some cardiovascular work into your circuit. For example, shuttle runs, sidestepping or skipping can be included. This will ensure that your heart rate is up and you are working on your fitness as well as your strength during your circuit.

Core stability should also be a major part of your strength program. When I refer to stability, I mean abdominal stability. This is different from abdominal strength, which is achieved through sit-ups and manifests itself in washboard abs! Abdominal stability is gained from teaching the muscles in the abdomen and back to hold your trunk in the correct position. This is important for posture and your ability to cope with a weights program later on. Further, abdominal stability can lead to increased speed and agility as it allows your body to work in a more efficient manner and expend less energy moving from one point to another.

As someone who suffers from a chronic lower-back injury, caused initially by poor posture and limited flexibility, this is probably the most important part of my training. There are many exercises that can be done to improve trunk stability.

Each of the following exercises is designed to work the stomach muscles. In order to do this, you should pull your belly button in towards your back and hold that position during each of the exercises. Stop the exercise the moment you are no longer able to hold the muscle contraction as there is no benefit in continuing. When you can no longer hold the position, you have found your limit and you should use that as a base level from which to improve.

Trunk stabilisation

Lie on your back with both knees bent and your feet flat on the ground. Pull your belly button in towards your back and hold. To start with, try to hold this position for fifteen seconds at a time. Rest for fifteen seconds, then repeat. Try to do ten of these. Gradually increase the length of time spent holding the muscle contraction.

Straight leg raise

Lie on your back with one leg bent and your foot flat on the ground. Lock the other knee so your leg is straight and slowly lift your straight leg fifteen to twenty centimetres off the floor. Hold your leg off the floor for ten seconds. Repeat ten times. Try to double the length of time you hold the position every couple of weeks and reduce the repetitions. Aim eventually to do four one-minute repetitions.

Advanced straight-leg raise

As above, but this time keep the foot of the bent leg five centimetres off the floor. Repeat as above.

Double-leg raise

Lie on your back with both knees bent and your feet flat on the ground. Slowly lift both feet off the ground and extend your legs so that your knees are at a 90° angle and hold this position for ten seconds. Rest for thirty seconds, and repeat ten times. Try to double the length of time you hold the position every couple of weeks, reducing the repetitions. Aim to eventually hold the position for at least two minutes.

Advanced double-leg raise

As above, but this time, when both feet are off the ground, hold and then gradually straighten one leg out, hold it for five seconds and then return it to its original position. Repeat with the other leg. This makes one repetition. Start off by doing ten repetitions with twenty seconds' rest between each one. Gradually reduce the rest time so that eventually you can do ten repetitions in a row.

Bridging

Lie on your back with both knees bent and your feet flat on the ground. Keep your head and shoulders on the floor and lift your hips off the ground until your shoulders, hips and knees are in a straight line. Hold this position for ten seconds. Rest, and repeat ten times. Try to double the length of time the position is held every couple of weeks, reducing the repetitions. Aim to eventually hold the position for at least two minutes.

Advanced bridging

As above, then slowly straighten one knee. Hold this position for ten seconds. Rest, and repeat with the other leg. Do the exercise ten times. Try to double the length of time you hold the position every couple of weeks, reducing the repetitions. Aim to eventually hold the position for at least one minute on each leg.

Reverse bridging

Start with your elbows and knees on the ground. Slowly drop your hips until your knees, hips and shoulders are in a straight line. Hold this position for ten seconds. Rest, and repeat ten times. Try to double the length of time the position is held every couple of weeks, reducing the repetitions. Aim to eventually hold the position for at least one minute.

Advanced reverse bridging

As above, but this time start on your toes, rather than your knees.

As well as doing these exercises as part of our strength training, the Swifts do four or five of these exercises at the conclusion of our pre-season endurance sessions. The advantage of this is that we get our muscles used to maintaining our core stability even when they are fatigued, as they would be in a netball game.

An excellent device for improving abdominal stability is the Swiss ball. These balls are like big beach balls only much stronger, and the idea is to perform certain exercises using the ball to promote both stability and flexibility. They are available in most sports stores and they range in price from $30 to $50. Make sure that you get a ball that suits your size and that it comes with a booklet of exercises. Your physiotherapist will also be able to provide you with some specific exercises and stretches.

Speed and Agility

Speed and agility sessions are vital components of a netball player's pre-season as they include specific preparation for a game situation. Speed and agility can be maintained throughout the off-season and in the first stage of the pre-season through cross-training. Regular games of sports such as squash, basketball, touch football and tennis are excellent ways to maintain your speed and agility, as you are working in short, sharp bursts and having fun at the same time.

The second stage of the pre-season should see you start sprint sessions which involve some technique work and longer sprints. The reason the sprints are longer than the distance you would normally sprint on a netball court is so that you have enough time to work on your technique during the sprint. By the time you move into five- and ten-metre bursts in the final stage of pre-season your sprinting technique needs to be spot-on so that you can reach maximum speed over a short distance as you would in a game.

In the third and final stage of the pre-season, you should be ready for some short sprints and also for the introduction of agility work.

It is absolutely essential that sprint and agility sessions are preceded by a thorough warm-up. There is the potential for injury to occur during these sessions as you will be working in bursts of 100 per cent effort.

Along with your usual warm-up, you should include a couple of extra run-throughs so you are ready for the intensive effort of a sprint or agility session.

Each sprint session should be structured roughly as follows.

▶ Active warm-up: This should take about fifteen to twenty minutes and consist of a five-minute jog, five to ten minutes of stretching and the dynamic warm-up outlined on pages 37–39. The warm-up should end with a couple of full court runs at about 75 per cent effort.

▶ Sprint warm-up: This should take ten to fifteen minutes and consist of exercises designed to work on sprint technique and to get the body ready to carry out the sprint drills.

▶ Sprint drills: This should take about ten minutes and consist purely of sprint work. The length of the sprint and the number of repetitions carried out will vary between the pre-season and competition phases.

▶ Warm-down: This should take fifteen to twenty minutes and consist of thorough stretching exercises.

Agility sessions are structured fairly similarly, with the sprint warm-up and sprint drills being substituted for agility drills.

To build your sprint sessions, choose three or four activities from the sprint warm-up section and finish off with the sprint drills relevant to the phase of training you are in. Similarly, build your agility sessions by choosing four or five activities from the agility drills section and slot them in between the active warm-up and warm-down.

Sprint Warm-up

50 metre run-throughs

Vary the speed during the run-through by sprinting ten metres at 90 per cent speed; ten metres at 100 per cent; ten metres at 90 per cent; ten metres at 100 per cent; and ten metres slowing down. Do this four times.

Quick feet

Jog for ten metres, then take as many small steps as possible for ten metres. Repeat. The aim of the drill is to get your feet turning over quickly and to cover the ten metres of small steps as fast as possible. Do five sets of these.

Stair sprinting

Sprint up a set of stairs. Do two sets stepping onto each stair with one foot, then two sets stepping onto each stair with both feet. Ensure that you alternate the lead leg each time. Do four lots of fifteen to twenty steps.

Uphill sprinting

You will only need a slight slope for this. Sprinting uphill will strengthen your sprint technique as you will have to work harder to maintain it while running uphill. Do four repetitions of fifteen metres.

Downhill sprinting

Again you will only need a slight downhill slope. Sprinting downhill will help to increase your foot speed as you will be forced to take lots of small, quick steps to keep up with the momentum you gain as you sprint down the slope. Do four repetitions of fifteen metres.

Lateral cone hops and sprint

Start by standing next to a small cone with your feet together. Jump left and right over the cone six times then sprint forward for ten metres. Do this four times.

Stop and go

Sprint for three to five steps, stop dead and go again. Do this three or four times over twenty metres. This drill is even better if you have a partner or supervisor calling 'stop' and 'go'. Do this five times.

Sprint Drills

The sprint drills are performed in sets and repetitions. The repetitions are the number preceding 'by'. So for example 'eight by ten metres' means carry out eight repetitions of ten-metre sprints. Each of the sprint drills should be carried out at 100 per cent effort.

Work on the start of the sprint during these drills by changing your starting position every couple of repetitions. For example, if you are doing five repetitions you might mix up your starts. Do one with your feet shoulder-width apart and standing on the balls of your feet; one with one foot forward and one back, and standing on the balls of your feet; one while pitter-pattering; one while facing backwards or sidewards; and one lying on your stomach and scrambling up into a sprint.

Other variations you may want to use include lying on your back, jumping, sidestepping and dodging before you sprint.

In the pre-season sessions you should concentrate on your sprint technique. Keep your hips forward and your body standing tall, drive your arms hard and take lots of small steps, particularly as you accelerate. Try to keep your feet hitting the ground slightly in front of your body rather than underneath or behind it, as this will drive your body forward and help you to stay tall. Finally, try to make your first step a forward one. It sounds ridiculous, but it is tempting to make your first step on a sprint a backwards one, particularly if someone is calling when to go. To overcome this, concentrate on driving your leg forward on your first step.

Pre-season — first stage

❱ Crosstraining — play tennis, squash, touch football or basketball.

Pre-season — second stage

❱ Two sets of four by twenty metre sprints.
❱ Two sets of four by fifteen metre sprints — add one repetition per week until you have a maximum of six.
❱ Walk back for recovery and rest for one to two minutes between sets.

Pre-competition

❱ Three sets of five by ten metre sprints — add one repetition per week until you have a maximum of seven.
❱ Walk back for recovery and rest for one to two minutes between sets.

Competition

❱ One set of five by ten metre sprints.
❱ One set of ten by five metre sprints — with five-metre sprints you don't have much time to get to reach 100 per cent speed, so it is important that you work on taking small steps at the start to quickly build some speed up.
❱ Walk back for recovery and rest for one to two minutes between sets.

Agility Drills

5 — 0 — 5 drill

Place three cones in a straight line, each five metres apart. Start at the middle cone, sprint forwards and touch the front cone. Run backwards, turn 180° at the middle cone to sprint forward to touch the second cone and run backwards to the middle. That is one repetition. Do two repetitions of three sets. Rest for one minute between sets.

5 — 0 — 5 sidestep

Same as above, but this time start facing to the side. Sidestep to the front cone, touch it and sidestep back to the middle. At the middle cone, turn 180° and sidestep to the second cone, touch it and sidestep back to the middle. That is one repetition. Do two repetitions of three sets. Rest for one minute between sets.

Shadows

This requires two people. Place four cones in a five-metre square. One player is the leader (player A) and one is the follower (player B). Player A starts anywhere in the square and player B starts within an arm's length of her. During the work period, player A runs anywhere in the square to try to get away from player B. Player B must 'shadow' player A and keep her within arm's length. Do two repetitions with each player as player A. Work for ten seconds with fifty seconds of rest.

T-drill

Place three cones in a straight line, each five metres apart. Place a fourth cone five metres in front of the middle cone so that the cones make a 'T' shape. Start at the middle cone, facing towards the single cone out in front. Stay facing forward and sprint to the cone on your left, touch it, and sprint to the cone on your right. Touch the cone on your right and sprint back to the middle. When you get back to the middle, sprint forwards, touch the front cone and run backwards to the start. Do three repetitions.

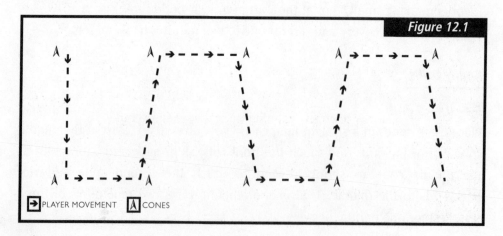

Figure 12.1

PLAYER MOVEMENT   CONES

In and out sprints

Place ten cones each five metres apart, as shown in Figure 12.1. Sprint in a forward direction to each cone, changing direction at each one. Do three repetitions.

Double triangles

Place seven cones each five metres apart, as shown in Figure 12.2. Sprint forward to each cone as indicated by the arrows. Do two repetitions sprinting to the left-hand side first, and two to the right-hand side. Once you are comfortable with sprinting forwards, try alternating between sidestepping and sprinting. For example, sprint to the first cone, sidestep to the second, sprint to the third, sidestep to the fourth and so on. Do four repetitions.

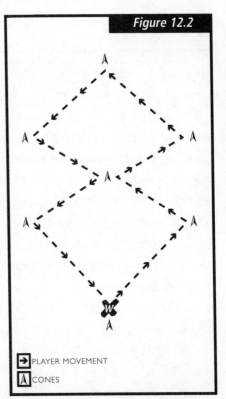

Figure 12.2

→ PLAYER MOVEMENT
Λ CONES

Top Tips

1. Sprint and agility sessions can be performed as a warm-up to court-work sessions.
2. You can vary the agility drills by making up your own patterns of cones to run through.
3. When doing agility exercises, it is important that you sprint between the cones as fast as you can so that you get used to changing direction at top speed.
4. You should try to sprint at 100 per cent effort for the full distance of each of your sprints. Don't fall into the trap of slowing down or stopping before you cover the full distance.

Testing

In order to determine whether your conditioning program is working, it is necessary to test its different components to see whether you are improving.

The Australian Netball Team undergo rigorous fitness tests several times a year. These tests check our height and weight, and measure our speed, agility, strength, vertical jump and endurance. The reason for the testing is not to see who is fit enough to be in the Australian team, but rather, to help our coach and our strength and conditioning trainer identify what areas we need to work on for the coming season. It also provides feedback as to whether our conditioning program is, in fact, working.

Our testing generally takes place under the supervision of the institute of sport in our home states, and uses specially designed machines to test our speed, agility and vertical jump. Strength is measured by a maximal bench press and squat test, and endurance is measured by a thing called the 'beep test'.

It is highly unlikely that your average netball team is going to have access to the type of facilities available at the various institutes of sport. You can, nevertheless, carry out your own fitness testing.

Speed

Time a thirty-metre sprint with a stopwatch. (Thirty metres is about the shortest distance you could time without the results being too greatly distorted by human error.)

Vertical jump

The player faces a wall and reaches up as high as she can with one hand. Make a mark with chalk on the player's fingertips. Rub some chalk on the player's fingertips and get her to jump as high as she can and touch the wall. The chalk on her fingertips will indicate the height of her jump. Her vertical jump is then measured by the distance between the reach height and the jump height. To ensure you get the best result, the player should perform three measured jumps. If you are testing more than one player, use different coloured chalk to avoid confusion.

Agility

Time the T-drill.

Endurance

There are a couple of ways to test endurance. The best way is the 'beep test'. This is a test where players do twenty-metre shuttle runs at a speed regulated by 'beeps' on a CD. The players must run the full twenty metres before the beep, and turn and run another twenty metres before the next beep. The beeps start off slowly for the first level, which is about a minute long, and get progressively faster for each level. The CDs containing the beep test are available from the Australian Sports Commission. They can be contacted on (02) 6214 1915.

The second test is simply measuring how far players can run in twelve minutes. It is less accurate, as the players will need to monitor their progress so that they are completely fatigued at the end of the twelve minutes, although it is easier than the beep test because you don't need any extra equipment. Ideally, this test should be done on a 400-metre oval. Simply record how many laps each player does in twelve minutes.

Testing should be carried out at the very start of the pre-season, which will then give you a base level of fitness. If you adhere to your strength and conditioning program, you should notice an improvement each time you are tested.

Chapter 13

Recovery

Recovery is an important part of the netball season. It is something the Sydney Swifts and the Australian Netball Team work hard at, as it is important that we keep our bodies in good condition throughout the season. It is something that takes on particular importance in the Australian team when we attend major events such as the Commonwealth Games or the World Netball Championships. As these competitions are generally played over the course of one to two weeks, with a game every day, it is vital that we recover well from each game so that we can come back and play well the following day.

It is not only matches that we must 'recover' from, but training sessions as well. It is important that we look after our bodies at the end of each training session so that we can get the most out of our next session, or so that we are in peak condition for the upcoming game.

Believe it or not, recovery actually starts before each session or match, through hydration. You must ensure that you drink plenty of water before and during each session or match so that you are not dehydrated when you finish.

Keeping hydrated will assist your body in getting over the fatigue associated with training for and playing netball.

The most basic — and indeed important — form of recovery from a match or training session is an 'active rest' activity such as a slow jog or walk, followed by stretching. The Australian team finish off each training session and most matches by slowly jogging for four laps of the court and then walking for four laps. We then carry out a good, long stretch for ten to fifteen minutes. We go through each of our muscle groups, holding each stretch for twenty to thirty seconds. If we have time, we do each stretch twice.

It is absolutely vital that you carry out some form of warm-down at the conclusion of every training session or match. This will help your body to recover from these strenuous activities as well as preventing injury. If you go into a session or match with tight muscles from previous sessions or matches, then you run the risk of further straining those muscles or injuring another part of your body because you are overcompensating for the muscles that are already tight.

During this time, we make sure that we put back some of the fuel that training or a match has taken out. This involves rehydrating, often with a glucose sports drink that replaces energy. We also eat something small, to replace some carbohydrates and protein. Post-training and post-match snacks include fresh fruit such as bananas, apples and oranges, as well as dried fruit, bread rolls, muffins, glucose lollies and cereal bars. It is possible to eat too much at the end of training or a match, so I tend to have a little bit of a lot of things. For example, a couple of glucose lollies, a few pieces of fruit, a cereal bar and half a bread roll are generally enough for me, as well as plenty of rehydrating drinks.

It is also important to eat something a bit more substantial within an hour of finishing a session. This meal should contain some more carbohydrates as well as some protein.

Both the Australian team and the Sydney Swifts take further action as part of our warm-down and recovery process to reduce muscle swelling and fatigue. Australian Institute of Sport scientist Angie Calder has carried out extensive research which suggests that cold water immersion, or hot and cold water contrast, is extremely beneficial to the recovery process.

Cold water immersion is a way of cooling muscles and reducing muscle swelling. It is the favoured method of the Australian team and the Sydney Swifts for recovering from matches. It involves filling a bath or a large garbage bin with cold water and a couple of bags of ice. Angie Calder recommends that the water is between 10° and 16°C. We stand in bins or sit in baths for one minute, then step out and lightly massage our legs for one minute. We repeat this process three times.

In case you were wondering, this is much more painful than playing a game of netball, and it is not something that I would recommend unless you are playing at an elite level. Rather, I would recommend a milder version using cold water only to fill the bath or bin. Keep the ice for chilling your drinks!

Despite the discomfort, I believe that it is worth it. Despite what I think, it is worth noting that some people simply cannot cope with cold temperatures and for them the benefits may not outweigh the discomfort. So, if you are coaching a team, you should allow your players to decide whether they want to carry out the cold water recovery. As a precaution, the water in the bath or bin should be changed for each player and the bath or bin cleaned out. Players with open wounds, poor circulation, skin infections or viruses should not use cold water immersion as a recovery treatment.

The alternative to cold water immersion is hot and cold water contrast. This is achieved by standing in a shower and alternating between one to two minutes of hot water and thirty seconds of cold water. Carry out this process three times.

Another great recovery treatment is massage. Massages are not cheap, and they can seem a little indulgent, but a massage from a sports massage therapist will do wonders for your recovery. I try to have a rub once a fortnight during the season, and it is amazing the difference it makes. If you are unable to get a massage from a massage therapist, then it is possible to massage your own legs. Using massage or baby oil, or moisturising cream, gently run your fingertips or thumbs from the bottom of your calves to the top, concentrating on any sore spots. Do this a couple of times, and repeat around your shins and on your quadriceps (thighs) and hamstrings. Self-massage is useful for sore or tight muscles. If you are not sure whether your muscles are simply tight or if you are suffering from a muscle strain or tear, or a cork (where the muscle is damaged by a sharp blow from an opponent's elbow or knee), see your physiotherapist before carrying out any self-massage.

Finally, the best form of recovery is sleep. Regular and adequate sleep will allow your body to carry out most of its recovery. It is recommended that you try to keep your sleep patterns as regular as possible. Avoid long naps during the day and long sleep-ins on the weekend.

At the end of the day, how you recover is up to you. Listen to your body and, by a process of trial and error, figure out what suits you best. Each player will be different, and every person will respond better to different methods of recovery. The most important thing to remember is that recovery is as important to your training regime as strength and conditioning and court work.

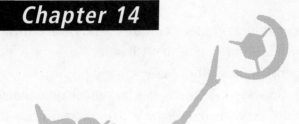

Chapter 14

Netball Nutrition

Your body is like a high-performance sports car: there are many components that you have to keep in good working order with regular maintenance and service checks. Just like a sports car, your body won't run on empty. You need to put fuel in it — but not just any old fuel. A high-performance engine requires high-performance fuel, and your body is no different.

People often ask me if I am on a special diet to help me play netball. The short answer to this is 'no'. The longer answer to this is that everyone has a 'diet', in so far as everyone has a certain pattern of eating. My 'diet' is essentially a balanced one. I eat very little, if any, take-away food or junk food such as chocolate or chips. Most of my energy comes from eating food that is high in carbohydrates, such as bread, cereal and pasta. I eat plenty of fruit and vegetables, and a moderate amount of protein such as meat, eggs and nuts as well as a reasonable amount of dairy food. I love yoghurt, milk and cheese, so I have no problem including a couple of servings of these a day in my diet, although I try to stick to low-fat alternatives. I don't steer completely clear of fats and oils, as these are necessary components of a healthy diet.

If you lumped together all of the food I go through in one day, you would see that I eat a fair amount, which is no surprise, really, as I have always been fairly good on the tooth! I am pretty fortunate that I have a high metabolism, which means that I tend to burn a lot of energy as I go through the day. As a result, I have never really had to watch what I eat. Nevertheless, I find that if I start eating junk or fatty foods, or start skipping meals, my energy levels plummet.

As well as eating food that is good for me, I also try to eat it in five or six small meals a day rather than three main meals. That may sound like a lot, but in actual fact, it is simply three smaller main meals supplemented with two or three snacks. This means that I have something to eat every three hours or so. A typical day for me would be a breakfast of fruit juice, cereal or porridge, and a couple of pieces of toast with a little bit of butter and either jam, peanut butter or Vegemite on top. I also like my cup of tea in the morning to help get me going. By mid-morning I get pretty hungry, so it is time for a tub of yoghurt or a piece of fruit. Lunch might be a ham and salad roll or pasta, with a mid-afternoon snack of either fruit or a muffin. Dinner is generally pasta, risotto, stir-fry, or some sort of meat with plenty of vegetables, including potatoes, which are high in carbohydrates. If I am still hungry after dinner, I will have some fruit or bread, and if I want to spoil myself then there is always ice cream in the freezer. My meals are also supplemented by fruit, muffins and glucose lollies when I am at training. If I am still hungry in-between times, then carrot and celery sticks are a great way to fill in the gaps.

Not only do you have to eat the right foods, you also have to drink the right drinks. I try to drink at least two litres of water every day, in addition to what I drink during training. I try to limit myself to two caffeine drinks a day and very little, if any, soft drink. Soft drinks are really high in sugar, so I rarely have them. If I feel like I need a sweetener, I stick to cordial or a diluted sports drink. If you can't do without soft drink, try to choose ones with a low sugar content, such as diet drinks.

The Australian team has a nutritionist, Kerry Leech, who helps us to structure our diets to meet our energy needs. If we feel we need to gain or lose weight, she is the lady we go to for advice on how to do this. On the whole, though, the best diet for a netball player is one that is balanced. So Kerry mostly gives us tips on what foods to choose and how to prepare them. The best tip I can pass on in terms of having a balanced diet is to be disciplined. It is pretty tempting to break into a packet of chips and a soft drink when your energy levels are low, but believe me, you will feel better if you choose a bottle of water and a muesli bar instead.

The best way to structure your diet is to choose from the five food groups. These are:

▶ fruit and vegetables;

▶ breads and cereals;

▶ meat and meat alternatives;

▶ dairy products; and

▶ fats and oils.

It is not only a matter of eating something every day from each of these food groups, but also of eating them in the right proportion. Typically, Western diets tend to contain too much fat and protein and not enough carbohydrates, fibre or vitamins and minerals. Main meals should contain plenty of carbohydrates and fibre in the form of rice, pasta, noodles, breads, cereals or potatoes. Carbohydrates are the most important energy source for exercise, and also for recovery. An adequate intake of carbohydrates will provide you with sufficient energy to get through training and matches.

Carbohydrates are important because they provide you with lots of slow-release energy. Unlike the quick energy burst and subsequent energy low you get from foods that are high in sugar, carbohydrate stores give you a long, sustained release of energy to help you get through training or a match, or a full day at school or work. Inadequate intakes will probably lead to you getting tired early in a match or training, losing concentration, and not recovering very well.

You should also include lots of vegetables and fruit in your daily food intake to ensure that you are getting sufficient vitamins and minerals. Vitamins and minerals not only help you perform better, but will also help you to maintain your overall health. Inadequate vitamin and mineral intakes may make you more susceptible to illness and slow down the speed at which you recover from injuries.

Protein is another vital component of a healthy diet, but it should be eaten in small quantities. At least one, and preferably two, small serves of protein should be eaten each day, which is as simple as having some chicken or ham on your sandwich at lunch, and a couple of serves of dairy food. The danger with many proteins is that they come with a high degree of fat. Fat is an essential part of the diet, but only in very small quantities. So try to choose low-fat dairy products, and remove any fat from meat and the skin from chicken. Doing this will remove most of the fat, while at the same time, leave enough to meet your daily requirements.

As well as taking in enough fuel in the right amounts, women in particular have to ensure they use their diets to guard against the effects of osteoporosis and anaemia.

Osteoporosis is a degenerative disease of the bones that tends to affect predominantly older women — although it can affect younger women and men if their diet is inadequate. To protect yourself from developing osteoporosis in your old age, it is necessary to eat at least three serves of dairy foods each day from a young age. Your bones will thank you for it.

Anaemia is a fancy word for low iron levels and the side effects associated with it. It is a common affliction among both women and athletes — so if you are a female athlete, beware! The symptoms of anaemia are feeling tired, breathlessness, cramps, and a low resistance to infection. The way to prevent anaemia is to ensure that you eat foods that are rich in iron, such as red meat, and in particular kidney and liver, as well as chicken and seafood. Eggs, cereals and bread are also good sources of iron. You can assist your body to absorb the iron in these foods by eating them in conjunction with a source of vitamin C, such as vegetables, fruit and juices.

All of this information sounds a bit daunting when you start to think about the dos and don'ts of nutrition. It may seem like an awful lot to remember, but it is, in fact, pretty simple — just eat sensibly and often! Small meals that are low in fat and high in carbohydrate are the way to go, along with plenty of fruit and vegetables.

This information should help you plan your overall diet, but what about eating for specific events? Most netballers will compete once a week, so it is easy to plan to have enough energy for your game. If you play on a Saturday, you should start to eat more high-carbohydrate foods and reduce your protein and fat intake towards the end of the week. An ideal meal on the night before a game would be pasta with a tomato-based sauce, stir-fry, risotto or some other rice-based dish. If you play your match before lunch, make sure that you have a good breakfast, such as cereal and toast, or pancakes with fruit and maple syrup.

If you play later in the day, or at night, your pre-match meal should be high in carbohydrates and be reasonably light. Pasta, rice, noodles or sandwiches are fine if they are not smothered in heavy sauces. Most of my Swifts team-mates prefer to eat fairly plain food before a game, so that their lunch doesn't repeat on them during the game. I differ slightly, in that, for some reason, I play better when I eat a pre-match meal that contains plenty of curry or chilli. I imagine that this is pretty unusual (my team-mates reckon it is just plain weird!), but it goes to show that everyone is different. At the end of the day, you need to find what works best for you.

If you are playing in a netball carnival that requires enough energy for several games in the one day, or across a weekend, you will need to start preparing several days beforehand. For sustained energy, during the week prior to the carnival choose at least one carbohydrate meal per day, such as pasta, rice or noodles. You should also drink plenty of water in the days prior so that you are really hydrated beforehand.

On competition days, eat plenty of food that is high in carbohydrates and contains plenty of glucose, as well as being easy to digest. Lollies such as jelly babies, snakes and frogs are perfect for glucose replacement — just make sure you don't eat too many! Sports drinks are also recommended as the glucose in them is easily and quickly absorbed into your system.

Carbohydrates are best replaced through eating fruit (both fresh and dried), bread and muffins. The banana muffin recipe at the end of this chapter is perfect for this. Tinned fruit is also a good idea because it is easy to pack and travels well. Try to steer clear of things like ice cream, chocolate, pies and sausage sandwiches. These are all easily available at netball carnivals but they will not fuel your body for your games.

So, the best way to get through a netball carnival is to drink often, and graze on easily digestible foods that will replace both glucose and carbohydrates. Stay away from foods that are high in fat and protein, and avoid eating large amounts of food at any one time.

Top Tips

1. *If you get nervous before a game and this results in an upset tummy or diarrhoea, try to choose foods that have less fibre in them.*
2. *Your pre-match preparation should include drinking plenty of water!*
3. *Don't forget post-match nutrition as well.*

Favourite Recipes

Two-minute noodles with tuna

This is one of my favourite snacks.

Cook a packet of two-minute noodles, discarding the flavour sachet.

Once they are cooked, serve with a tin of tuna. Try using flavoured tuna, such as tuna with dill, cracked pepper or chilli. This is really easy to make and good for you. To reduce the fat intake, use air-dried noodles.

Serves one

Banana Muffins

This is a recipe from the Australian team nutritionist, Kerry Leech.

You will need:

2 very ripe bananas	1 cup wholemeal self-raising flour
1 egg	1 cup white self-raising flour
½ cup low-fat milk	½ teaspoon ground cinnamon
½ cup apple juice	½ teaspoon baking powder

Preheat the oven to 200°C.

Mash the bananas until there are no lumps. Beat the egg and add it to the bananas. Add the milk and apple juice. Sift all of the flour, cinnamon and baking powder and fold into the liquid mixture. Mix well by hand.

Spoon the mixture into very lightly greased muffin tins, filling each up about two-thirds. Bake for approximately twenty minutes until lightly browned and cooked through. Cool on a cake rack.

Makes twelve

Stir-Fry

You will need:

500g lean beef, lamb, chicken or peeled prawns	2 baby bok choy
2 tablespoons green curry paste (less if you don't like hot food)	2 zucchini sliced into three-centimetre strips
1 small broccoli, cut into florets	½ cup chopped coriander
2 carrots, sliced into three-centimetre strips	1 tablespoon honey
1 capsicum (red or green), sliced into three-centimetre strips	1 tablespoon hoi sin sauce
any other 'hard' vegetables you want to include	1 tablespoon oyster sauce
	chilli to taste
	2 tablespoons soy sauce
	2 packets fresh noodles

Heat a non-stick wok to a reasonably high heat and add the meat or prawns. Stir in the green curry paste.

When the meat is cooked remove it from the wok. Add about half a cup of water to the wok and then add the broccoli, carrots, capsicum and any other 'hard' vegetables you may be using. Simmer the vegetables for approximately two minutes.

Add the remainder of the vegetables, and the coriander, honey, hoi sin and oyster sauce, and add chilli to taste. Stir for a couple of minutes until the vegetables are cooked.

Add extra water as required, so that there is always just enough water to stop the vegetables burning. They should be tender but not too soft or too crispy. Remove the vegetables from the wok. There should be a small amount of water left. Put the noodles and soy sauce in the wok for about thirty seconds. Return the vegetables and meat to the wok and toss with the noodles. Serve in large bowls.

Serves four

Pasta Surprise

You will need:

500g fettuccine	1 broccoli, cut into florets
5–6 slices prosciutto or ham, sliced into five-centimetre strips	1 bunch asparagus, cut in half
1 carton light sour cream	2 zucchini, sliced into three-centimetre strips

Cook the pasta according to the directions on the packet. Drain and set aside.

Heat a heavy, non-stick fry pan and cook the prosciutto until it just becomes crisp. Add the sour cream to the prosciutto and mix well. Stir the broccoli, asparagus, and zucchini into the sour cream. Reduce the heat, cover the fry pan and simmer until the vegetables are cooked.

To serve, divide the pasta into four bowls and top with the sauce.

Serves four

Chicken and Vegetable Risotto

You will need:

1 spanish onion, sliced lengthways
    into six to eight wedges
4 roma tomatoes, cut in half
12 spears of baby corn
3 zucchini, quartered
600g pumpkin, peeled and cut into
    three-centimetre chunks

1 cup white wine
4 cups chicken or vegetable stock
2 tablespoons olive oil
1 leek, chopped
500g chicken tenderloins
Cajun seasoning
2 cups Arborio rice

Place onion, tomatoes, corn, zucchini and pumpkin on a greased baking tray and roast at 200°C for forty minutes, or until pumpkin is cooked through.

Place wine and stock into a saucepan and simmer gently.

Heat the olive oil in a heavy-bottomed frypan or large saucepan, add the leek and cook until soft and golden. Add the chicken to the pan and sprinkle on the Cajun seasoning. Stir occasionally until chicken is cooked through.

Remove the chicken and leek, leaving as much of the meat juices in the pan as possible. Add the rice to the pan and stir until the rice looks 'polished'. Add the stock and wine mixture to the rice a cup at a time, stirring until the liquid is absorbed. Keep adding the liquid until the rice is soft and creamy. When the rice is cooked, add the chicken and leek and stir through.

To serve, divide the risotto between four bowls and top with the roasted vegetables.

Serves four

Liz Ellis would like to thank her sponsors

Kellogg's
CORN
FLAKES

2KY1017
BIG SPORTS BREAKFAST

HORSELL